"A First Book for Understanding Diabetes"
is a synopsis of the larger book,
"Understanding Diabetes."

W9-CFG-973

It provides a quick summary of each of the chapters.
It may be easier to begin learning from this book until you are
ready to read the larger book.

NOTES

13th Edition

A FIRST BOOK FOR UNDERSTANDING

DIABETES

A COMPANION BOOK TO "UNDERSTANDING DIABETES"

H. Peter Chase, MD
and
David M. Maahs, MD, PhD

A First Book for Understanding Diabetes, 13th Edition
Copyright ©2014
by H. Peter Chase and David M. Maahs

THE PINK PANTHER™ & ©1964-2014
Metro-Goldwyn-Mayer Studios Inc.
All Rights Reserved.
All "Pink Panther," "The Inspector" and other characters
are not to be reproduced without permission from Metro-Goldwyn-Mayer Studios Inc.

For Information, contact
Children's Diabetes Foundation at Denver, Colorado
4380 South Syracuse Street, Suite 430
Denver, CO 80237

www.ChildrensDiabetesFoundation.org

Library of Congress Control Number 2014937500

ISBN 9780983265047

Published by
Children's Diabetes Foundation at Denver, Colorado
4380 South Syracuse Street, Suite 430   Denver, CO 80237
303-863-1200

Book Design by Cindy Kalkofen

Printed in the United States of America
by American Web

THIS BOOK IS DEDICATED TO THE MANY PEOPLE WITH DIABETES WHO HAVE CONTRIBUTED THEIR TIME AND EFFORT PARTICIPATING IN RESEARCH STUDIES IN ORDER TO ADVANCE OUR KNOWLEDGE ABOUT DIABETES.

SPECIAL THANKS TO...

The staff of the Children's Diabetes Foundation.

Hannah Goettle, Regina Reece, Emily Westfall,
for manuscript preparation, editing and proofreading.

Cindy Kalkofen for book design, graphics, and illustrations.

MGM Consumer Products for allowing the use of THE PINK PANTHER™.
www.pinkpanther.com

Additional copies of this publication may be purchased from the Children's Diabetes Foundation at Denver. See available publications at the end of this book.

TABLE OF CONTENTS

THE CHAPTERS IN THIS BOOK
FOLLOW THE CHAPTERS IN
"UNDERSTANDING DIABETES."

CHAPTER 1
THE IMPORTANCE OF EDUCATION IN DIABETES

It is important to learn all about diabetes. At the time of diagnosis the family will spend one to three days learning about diabetes. Early education will focus on initial survival skills. Approximately one week later they will return for another day. This book will help in the beginning, until the family is ready to read the larger book, "*Understanding Diabetes.*" In both books, the chapters have the same numbers and topics. All family members, including both parents, should be present for initial education. In this book we use "you" for you and your child.

Initial teaching (survival skills) often includes:

- □ What diabetes is and what causes it
- □ Urine and/or blood ketone checking
- □ Blood sugar checking
- □ Recognizing a low blood sugar and how to treat it
- □ Insulin types and actions
- □ Drawing up insulin
- □ Giving shots
- □ Food survival skills

In addition to survival skills, other areas often covered are:

- □ A school plan
- □ When to call your diabetes care-provider
- □ Details of treatment (including "thinking" scales)
- □ Education about food (dietitian)
- □ Feelings (psych-social team)
- □ Plans for the next few days

One-Week Follow Up

Usually at one week the family and child return for group education with other families. The content includes teaching done by the dietitian and nurse and a clinic visit with the physician, a nurse practitioner or physician-assistant. Areas covered include:

- □ Details of food management with diabetes
- □ Review of HbA1c: what is it, why is it important
- □ Insulin actions and different insulin regimens
- □ Pattern management of blood sugars: how to identify trends and when to fax or email numbers (all families are given fax sheets to send in weekly until blood sugars and insulin doses stabilize)
- □ Low blood sugar care: causes, signs and treatment of mild to severe low blood sugars including a review of the use of glucose tablets and gel and the administration of glucagon
- □ High blood sugar care: prevention of diabetic ketoacidosis; causes, signs and treatment
- □ Sick-day management: how often to check blood sugars and ketones, fluid replacement — what type and how much, when and how to urgently call for assistance

THE IMPORTANCE OF EDUCATION IN DIABETES

Special instructions for the first night are summarized below.

A. *The diabetes supplies you will need the first night include* (your nurse will mark which you need):

    ____ Blood glucose meter   ____ Meter glucose strips   ____ Alcohol swabs

    ____ Ketone check strips   ____ Glucose gel & tabs   ____ Log book

    ____ Insulin   ____ Syringes   ____ Phone card

The first night you will either get your insulin injection at our clinic, or you will give the shot at home or where you are staying.

B. *If the insulin is given while at the clinic:*

1. If Humalog®/NovoLog® or Apidra® insulin has been given, eat in 15-20 minutes (or have a snack if blood sugar below 100 mg/dL [<5.5 mmol/L]).

2. If Regular insulin has been given, try to eat your meal in 30 minutes – or have a snack containing carbohydrates if it will be more than 30 minutes.

3. Eat until the appetite is satisfied, avoiding high sugar foods (especially regular sugar pop [soda], other sweetened drinks, juice and sweet desserts).

C. *If the dinner insulin is to be given at home:*

1. Check the blood sugar right before the injection. Enter the result into the log book.

2. Check for urine ketones.

3. Call _____ at _____ or page at _____ for an insulin dose Give this dose: _____.

4. Draw up and give the insulin injection 15-20 minutes before the meal (give at mealtime if below 100 mg/dL [<5.5 mmol/L]). If you are not very hungry, or are too tired to eat, call the diabetes care team with any dose questions.

D. *Before Bed:*

1. Check the blood sugar. Enter the result into the log book.

2. Check for urine or blood ketones.

3. Call your physician at the numbers listed above if the blood sugar is below ____ or above ____, or if urine ketones are "moderate" or "large" or if blood ketones are >0.6 mmol/L. If urine ketones are "trace" or "small," drink 8-12 oz of water before going to bed.

4. Give an insulin injection if your diabetes care team instructs you to do so (dose, if ordered = _____).

5. Eat a bedtime snack. This may not always be needed in the future, but the insulin dose is still being adjusted. Some ideas for this snack include: cereal and milk, toast and peanut butter, a slice of pizza, yogurt and graham crackers, or cheese and crackers.

E. *The next morning:*

1. Check the blood sugar and the urine ketones upon awakening (if blood sugar is less than 70 mg/dL [3.9 mmol/L], drink 4–6 oz of juice promptly).

2. If your physician has instructed you to give the morning insulin at home, then follow your insulin dosing plan (see Table). Follow the steps listed above (see letter "C") for last night's meal dose if you have questions.

3. If you have been instructed to wait to give the morning dose until after coming to the clinic, check the blood sugar and the urine ketones upon awakening (if blood sugar is less than 70 mg/dL [3.9 mmol/L], drink 4-6 oz of juice promptly).

4. If you are coming/returning to the clinic the next day, you may be asked to do any of the options below.

    ☐ Take your insulin shot at home (as above) and eat breakfast before coming.

    ☐ Eat breakfast at home, and then come to the clinic for your insulin injection.

    ☐ Bring your breakfast to the clinic, and eat it after the insulin has been given.

    ☐ Bring all blood checking supplies and materials you received the first day back to the clinic (including your log book, Pink Panther book, insulin and supplies).

TABLE

Insulin Injection Dosing – Onset Day 2*						
	Blood Sugar mg/dL (mmol/L)	A.M.	Lunch	P.M.	Dinner	Bedtime
A) Long-Acting Insulin _____						
B) Intermediate-Acting Insulin (NPH) _____						
C) Rapid-Acting Insulin (sliding scale) _____	70-150 (3.9-8.3)					
	150-250 (8.3-13.9)					
	250-350 (13.9-19.4)					
	350-450 (19.4-25.0)					
	>450 (2.5)					

*This Table will be filled out by your diabetes care-provider if he or she has instructed.
Above 300 mg/dL or 16.7 mmol/dL, call diabetes care-provider after ketones checked.

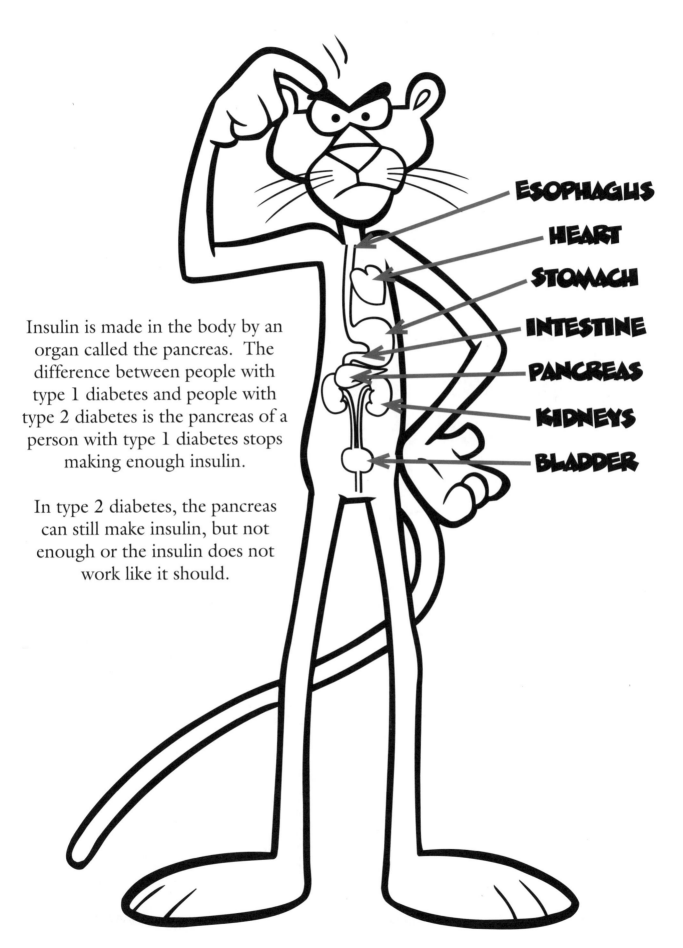

ESOPHAGUS

HEART

STOMACH

INTESTINE

PANCREAS

KIDNEYS

BLADDER

Insulin is made in the body by an organ called the pancreas. The difference between people with type 1 diabetes and people with type 2 diabetes is the pancreas of a person with type 1 diabetes stops making enough insulin.

In type 2 diabetes, the pancreas can still make insulin, but not enough or the insulin does not work like it should.

Chapter 1 – The Importance of Education in Diabetes

Type 1 diabetes (Childhood, Juvenile, Insulin-dependent diabetes) is due to not enough insulin being made in the pancreas (see picture and Chapter 3). The most common signs are:

- **frequent passing of urine (polyuria)**

- **constant thirst (polydipsia)**

- **weight loss**

For people with type 1 diabetes, insulin must be taken by injection. Insulin cannot be taken as a pill because the stomach acid would destroy it.

Type 2 diabetes (Adult-onset, or Non-insulin dependent diabetes) is different from type 1 diabetes (see Chapter 4). Although the above symptoms may be present, there are often no symptoms at diagnosis. Insulin is still made, but not enough, or it doesn't work very well. People with type 2 diabetes can sometimes use pills (which are not insulin) and diet and exercise to control their diabetes (see Chapter 4). Eating healthy food and exercising are also important for people with type 1 diabetes, but they will always need to take insulin shots.

Insulin allows sugar to pass into our cells to be used for energy. It also turns off the body's making of sugar. When not enough insulin is present, the sugar cannot pass into the body's cells. The sugar is high in the blood and it passes out in the urine. Frequent passing of urine is the result. (See Figures on the next 2 pages.) A goal of treatment is to give insulin back to the person as needed to replace the insulin they are unable to make.

Because sugar cannot be used for energy without insulin, the body breaks down fat for energy. **Ketones** are the result of using fat for energy.

When insulin treatment begins, the urine/blood ketones gradually disappear (see Chapter 5). After a few days, the blood sugars come into range and the excess passing of urine and drinking of water will decrease. Weight is gained back, the appetite normalizes and the person starts to feel much better.

Pre-diabetes refers to the period before developing diabetes. It is usually detected in people who will develop type 1 diabetes because they have had the blood test to detect islet cell antibodies (see Chapters 3 and 32). Pre-type 2 diabetes is very common. It is usually diagnosed in people who are overweight and who have borderline blood sugar and/or HbA1c levels (see Chapter 14). Weight loss and exercise can help delay or prevent the onset of type 2 diabetes (but not type 1 diabetes).

DIABETES

Liver

No insulin to shut off **internal** sugar production

Sugar

Bridge

Stomach

Sugar

Hungry Cell

No Insulin

External sugar from our food

Sugar

Sugar

Sugar in urine

Sugar

No energy from sugar

WHAT HAPPENS TO SUGAR IN A PERSON WITH DIABETES

THE MYSTERY OF WHAT CAUSES TYPE 1 DIABETES
IS NOW BETTER UNDERSTOOD.

CHAPTER 3
TYPE 1 DIABETES

WHAT CAUSES DIABETES?

The cause of type 1 diabetes is believed to be due to three things: genetics, self-allergy and possibly a virus (or other stimulant).

GENETICS (INHERITANCE)

Genes come from both mom and dad and can make someone more likely to get diabetes. Over half of the people that get type 1 diabetes have inherited the gene combination DR3/DR4 (one is from mom and one is from dad).

SELF-ALLERGY (AUTOIMMUNITY)

- The immune system protects the body from possible harm, such as from an infection.

- An allergy is a reaction by the body's immune system to something it thinks doesn't belong inside the body.

- Self-allergy (autoimmunity) is when a person's body develops an allergy against one of its own parts. In this case, the allergy is against the islet ('eye-let') cells in the pancreas where insulin is made. When the islet cells have been damaged, the immune system makes something called antibodies. These antibodies are present in the blood and are markers of the immune system attacking the pancreas.

Antibodies that may be found in the blood of people with type 1 diabetes are:

- IAA (insulin autoantibody)
- GAD antibody
- ICA512 antibody

- ZnT8 antibody
- Islet cell antibodies (by fluorescent stain)

Sometimes these antibodies are present for many years before the signs of diabetes appear. Being able to identify antibodies has allowed studies to try to prevent type 1 diabetes (see Chapter 32 on research).

VIRUS (OR OTHER STIMULANT)

Having a certain gene makeup may allow a virus or other stimulant (currently unknown) to get to the islet cells (where insulin is made) and cause damage. Once the damage has occurred, the self-allergy likely begins.

DIAGNOSIS AND TREATMENT

The **symptoms** of diabetes have been discussed in Chapter 2. The **treatment** of type 1 diabetes is always with insulin (Chapter 8). Frequent blood sugar checking (Chapter 7) is important. Following a food plan (Chapter 12) and daily exercise (Chapter 13) are also important.

Often a **"honeymoon"** time begins a few weeks or months after a person with type 1 diabetes starts insulin shots. The insulin dose may go down and it may seem like the person does not have diabetes, but **THEY DO!** This period may last from a few weeks to a few years.

Checking **blood sugars** at least four times per day is essential for people with type 1 diabetes. The eventual use of an insulin pump (Chapter 28) or a continuous glucose monitor (CGM; Chapter 29) may help make diabetes management easier.

11

THIRTY TO SIXTY MINUTES OF EXERCISE
AT LEAST FIVE TIMES A WEEK IS IMPORTANT
FOR PEOPLE WITH DIABETES.

Type 2 diabetes (previously referred to as Adult-onset diabetes or Non-insulin dependent diabetes) is the most common type to occur in adults over age 40 years. It is also becoming more common in youth (particularly in overweight teenagers). Native-American, African-American and Latino youth have an increased risk for type 2 diabetes.

CAUSES

Type 2 diabetes is partly inherited (genetic). It is also linked with being overweight and not getting enough exercise. It is often called a "disease of life-styles." Our ancestors were very active and ate less. We now live in a world of automobile travel, television, computers, video games, and high calorie fast foods.

Type 2 (Adult-onset) diabetes does not occur as a result of the self-allergy like type 1 diabetes. Therefore, the antibodies (found in type 1 diabetes) are not present in the blood. Type 2 diabetes is often associated with being overweight.

People with type 2 diabetes may have normal or high insulin levels. Being overweight leads to "insulin resistance." The insulin just does not work well. In contrast, people with type 1 diabetes have low or no insulin. The two conditions are both called diabetes. Both result in high sugar levels, but the causes are VERY different from each other.

SYMPTOMS

The symptoms can be the same as with type 1 diabetes (Chapter 2). They may be:

- frequent drinking of liquids

- frequent urination (going to the bathroom)

- infections

- sores that heal slowly

- no energy

Many people don't have any symptoms. These people are sometimes diagnosed by a high blood sugar that is measured on a routine physical exam or with an elevated hemoglobin A1c (HbA1c) level (see Chapter 14). Others are diagnosed when they have a high blood sugar level during an Oral Glucose Tolerance Test (see "*Understanding Diabetes*," Chapter 4).

TREATMENT: CHANGES IN LIFESTYLE ARE <u>VERY</u> IMPORTANT.

- Eating foods with fewer calories and carbohydrates as well as less fat is very important.

- Getting at least 60 minutes of exercise five to seven days a week is important.

- Checking blood sugars (like people with type 1 diabetes) is helpful (Chapter 7). The blood sugar values can tell how well the person is doing.

- The HbA1c level tells how high blood sugar levels have been for every second of the day for the past three months and should be measured every 3 months (see Chapter 14). The level reflects the likelihood of later diabetes complications (Chapter 23).

- If at diagnosis a person has ketones, or very high blood sugar or HbA1c values, insulin shots are usually needed. The shots may also be needed during times of illness.

- Medications by mouth can be tried if the blood sugar and HbA1c levels return to near normal (Chapter 14). Often, by losing weight and exercising, blood sugar levels do return to near normal.

- The medicines taken by mouth ARE NOT insulin. When taken, these medicines may cause the pancreas to make more insulin. They can also make the body more sensitive to its own insulin. Some medicines also cause the liver to release less sugar into the blood.

- One of these medicines is called **metformin (Glucophage®)**.

- This medicine is usually tried first.

- Rarely, it can cause an upset stomach. Starting with lower doses and gradually increasing the dose often helps.

- If a person becomes sick, this medicine should be stopped until they are well. Blood sugars and urine ketones should be checked. Insulin shots may be needed during the illness. Call your doctor or nurse if you are not sure what to do.

- There are other medicines taken by mouth that can be tried if metformin isn't working well.

- We are learning more about type 2 diabetes in adolescents from the TODAY study. Over a period of three years, half of the patients needed insulin in order to control their blood sugar levels.

Checking ketones is very easy and very important.

A. FOR A NEWLY DIAGNOSED PERSON

The first goal for new patients is to clear their ketones.

Ketones come from fat breakdown. Insulin stops fat breakdown and prevents ketones from being made.

A second goal is to lower blood sugar levels.

Insulin also turns off sugar production from the liver and allows sugar to enter the body's cells (see Figures in Chapter 2).

B. FOR A PERSON WITH KNOWN DIABETES

When to check for ketones (either in urine or blood):

• during any illness

• with a very high blood sugar (e.g., above 300 mg/dL [>16.7 mmol/L])

• if an insulin shot is missed

• after vomiting even once

• with a blockage of an insulin pump catheter or pump failure

If ketones are present, extra insulin can be given to stop the ketones from being made. (Ketones need to be detected early and extra insulin given or the person may get very sick; see Chapter 15 on diabetic ketoacidosis [DKA].)

C. HOW TO CHECK FOR KETONES

A method to check for ketones must always be in the home and taken along on trips. Checking ketones and giving extra insulin can help prevent the person from becoming very sick. Ketones can be checked using either urine or a drop of blood. The urine strips are cheaper, although the blood has the advantage of telling how high the ketones are at that moment. Some people do the urine ketone check first, and only do the blood ketones if the urine shows moderate or large ketones.

URINE KETONES

The two main strips used are:

1. Ketostix®: This strip is dipped into the urine and is read as negative, trace, small, moderate, large, or extra large after *exactly* 15 seconds.

2. Chemstrip K®: This strip is dipped into the urine and is read as negative, trace, small, moderate, large or extra large after *exactly* 60 seconds. All urine ketones strips (including Ketostix) must be thrown out six months after the bottle is opened.

BLOOD KETONES

Some people prefer to use a meter to check blood ketones. There are now several meters for checking blood ketone levels. These include the Precision Xtra® (Abbott labs) and the Nova Max® ketone meter (Nova® Biomedical). For the Precision Xtra, the method is as follows:

- The blood ketone strip is inserted with the three black bars going into the meter.
- Then a drop of blood is placed on the white target area at the end of the strip.
- The result is given in 10 seconds.

COMPARISON OF BLOOD AND URINE KETONE READINGS

Blood Ketone (mmol/L)	Urine Ketone Strip color	Level	Action to take
less than 0.6	slight/no color change	negative	normal - no action needed
0.6 to 1.0	light purple	small to moderate	extra insulin & fluids**
1.1 to 3.0	dark purple	moderate to large*	call MD or RN**
greater than 3.0	very dark purple	very large*	go directly to the E.R.

*It is usually advised to call a healthcare-provider for a blood ketone level greater than 1.0 or with urine ketone readings of moderate or large.

**If the blood glucose level is below 150 mg/dL (<8.3 mmol/L), a liquid with sugar (e.g., juice) should be taken so more insulin can be safely given.

CHAPTER 6
LOW BLOOD SUGAR (HYPOGLYCEMIA OR INSULIN REACTION)

Anyone who has been given insulin can have low blood sugar (hypoglycemia or a "reaction"). Blood sugars below 70 mg/dL (3.9 mmol/L) are considered low and are usually related to the person having one or more of the signs outlined below. **A "true low" blood sugar is a value less than 60 mg/dL (3.3 mmol/L) which is a level not likely to occur in people who do not have diabetes or another disorder.** (Although "blood sugar" is used throughout this chapter, and in many of the chapters, if the person is using a continuous glucose monitor [CGM], it may be the "CGM glucose value." The terms "sugar" and "glucose" are used interchangeably in this book.)

MAIN CAUSES OF LOW BLOOD SUGAR:

• late or missed meals or snacks

• extra exercise (the low may be "delayed" during the night)

• too much insulin/wrong dose

• taking bath, shower or hot tub too soon after injection (dangerous)

• a previous low blood sugar (for any reason, particularly at bedtime) and failing to do a follow-up blood sugar 15 to 30 minutes later to make sure the value has come up as a result of the treatment ("hypoglycemia can cause further hypoglycemia")

• illnesses, especially with vomiting

• alcohol intake

FREQUENT SIGNS OF A LOW BLOOD SUGAR:

• hunger

• feeling shaky, sweaty and/or weak

• confusion

• sleepiness (at unusual times)

• behavioral/mood changes

• double vision

• the signs of nighttime lows may be the same, or may include waking up alert, crying, or having bad dreams

Low blood sugar can come on quickly. It must be treated immediately by the person (if able) or by someone who is nearby at the time. The **"rule of 15"** is to take 15 grams of rapid-acting carbohydrate (e.g., four dextrose tablets) and to recheck the blood sugar level in 15 minutes. It is important not to over-treat lows and raise the blood sugar level excessively. If not treated, eventual loss of consciousness or a seizure may occur. Different levels of reactions (mild, moderate, severe) and treatment for each level are discussed below and in the table in this chapter.

MILD, MODERATE AND SEVERE LOW BLOOD SUGAR

With a "mild" low blood sugar (also see Table), the following apply.

- Give sugar (best in liquid form) such as four ounces of juice or sugar pop. Dextrose tablets (four) also work.

- When possible, a blood sugar should be done.

- It takes 10 to 20 minutes for the blood sugar to rise after treatment.

- Re-check the blood sugar after 15 minutes to make sure the level is above 70 mg/dL (3.9 mmol/L).

- If it is still below this level, the liquid sugar or Dextrose tablets should be given again. Follow the steps above.

- Wait another 15 minutes to repeat the blood sugar level.

- If the blood sugar is above 70 mg/dL (3.9 mmol/L), consider giving solid food. The reason for waiting to give the solid food is that it may soak up the liquid sugar and slow the time for the sugar to get into the blood.

- The person should not return to activity until the blood sugar is above 70 mg/dL (3.9 mmol/L).

- If the low is at bedtime, it is important to repeat the blood sugar, as above, and again during the night to make sure the level stays up.

- If a low blood sugar occurs when it is time for an insulin shot, always treat the low first. Make sure the blood sugar is above 70 mg/dL (3.9 mmol/L) before giving the shot.

With a "moderate" reaction (also see Table), the following apply.

- Put half a tube of Insta-Glucose® or cake gel between the gums and cheeks. Rub the cheeks and stroke the throat to help with swallowing.

- If a person has a low blood sugar and can't keep food down or has difficulty getting the value up, **low dose glucagon**, one unit per year of age up to 15 units, can be given under the skin just like insulin - with an insulin syringe. The dose can be repeated every 20 minutes until the blood sugar is up. Once glucagon is mixed, it usually can continue to be used for about 24 hours before it gels.

With a "severe" reaction (also see Table), the following apply.

- If a seizure or complete loss of consciousness occurs, it is usually necessary to give a shot of glucagon.

- If no response in 10-15 minutes, may need to call 911.

- If on an insulin pump, remember to disconnect or suspend the insulin delivery.

- Your doctor or nurse should be called prior to the next insulin shot, as the amount of insulin you give may need to be changed.

GLUCAGON

- Glucagon will make the blood sugar rise, usually in 10 to 20 minutes. Although the result of giving glucagon is the opposite of giving insulin, it is <u>NOT</u> sugar.

- After mixing, glucagon can be given with an insulin syringe, just like insulin.

The amount of glucagon to give varies with age:

- Under 6 years: can be given a full 30 unit syringe (0.3 cc).

- 6-12 years: can be given a full 50 unit syringe (0.5 cc).

- Over 12 years: can be given a full 100 unit syringe (1.0 cc).

- If the person does not respond in 10 to 20 minutes, the paramedics (911) should be called.

- Instructions are simplified in the school setting (Chapter 25), with instructions to give 0.5 cc if <16 years old or 1.0 cc if ≥16 years old. It is important just to get some in.

- Glucagon should always be readily available and taken on trips. It will spoil if it freezes or gets above 90°F (32°C).

HYPOGLYCEMIA: TREATMENT OF LOW BLOOD SUGAR (B.S.)
ALWAYS CHECK BLOOD SUGAR LEVEL!

Low Blood Sugar Category	MILD	MODERATE	SEVERE
Alertness	<u>ALERT</u>	<u>NOT ALERT</u> **Unable to drink safely (choking risk)** Needs help from another person	<u>UNRESPONSIVE</u> **Loss of consciousness** **Seizure** **Needs constant adult help (position of safety)** ***Give nothing by mouth*** *(extreme choking risk)*
Symptoms	Mood Changes Shaky, Sweaty Hungry Fatigue, Weak Pale	Lack of Focus Headache Confused Disoriented 'Out of Control' (bite, kick) ***Can't*** Self-treat	Loss of Consciousness Seizure
Actions to take	• Check B.S. • Give 2-8 oz sugary fluid (amount age dependent) • Recheck B.S. in 10-15 min. • B.S. *<70 mg/dL (<3.9 mmol/L), repeat sugary fluid and recheck in 10-20 min. • B.S. *>70 mg/dL (>3.9 mmol/L), (give a solid snack) • Slight risk for more lows in next 24 hours (after any low blood sugar)	• ***Place in position of safety*** • Check B.S. • If on insulin pump, may disconnect or suspend until fully recovered from low blood sugar (**awake and alert**) • Give Insta-Glucose or cake decorating gel - put between gums and cheek and rub in • Look for person to 'wake up' • Recheck B.S. in 10-20 min. • ***Once alert*** – follow "actions" under 'Mild' column • Moderate risk for more lows in next 24 hours	• ***Place in position of safety*** • Check B.S. • If on insulin pump, disconnect or suspend until fully recovered from low blood sugar (**awake and alert**) • Glucagon: *can be given with an insulin syringe* like insulin: • Under 6 years: **30 units (3/10cc)** • 6-12 years: **50 units (1/2 cc)** • Over 12 years: **100 units (all of dose or 1 cc)** • If giving 50 or 100 unit doses, may use syringe in box and inject through clothing • **Check B.S. every 10-15 min. until *>70 mg/dL (>3.9 mmol/L)** • <u>**If no response, may need to call 911**</u> • **Check B.S. every hour for 4-5 hours** • High risk for more lows for 24 hours (need to increase food intake and decrease insulin doses)
Recovery time	10-20 minutes	20-45 minutes	**Call RN/MD** and report the episode. Effects can last 2-12 hours.

* < sign means "less than"   > sign means "greater than"

NEVER GIVE AN INSULIN SHOT AND THEN GET IN A SHOWER, BATHTUB OR HOT TUB. THE BLOOD COMING TO THE SKIN SURFACE MAY CAUSE THE INSULIN TO BE RAPIDLY ABSORBED. THIS MAY RESULT IN A SEVERE INSULIN REACTION.

IT IS IMPORTANT FOR ADULTS TO
KEEP AN EYE ON YOUNGER CHILDREN
FOR SIGNS OF LOW SUGAR.

IT IS IMPORTANT TO ALWAYS CHECK A BLOOD SUGAR BEFORE DRIVING.

Cotton Balls

Lancets

Meter

Test Strip

Finger Poker

CHECK YOUR BLOOD SUGARS (FOUR OR MORE TIMES EACH DAY) BEFORE EATING, EXERCISE AND BED.

CHAPTER 7
BLOOD SUGAR (GLUCOSE) MONITORING

Blood sugar checking involves obtaining a small sample of blood using a small lancing device ("poker"). A small drop of blood is placed on a disposable test strip. A meter is then used to calculate the amount of blood sugar in the sample. The blood sample is usually taken from a fingertip. Some people use an "alternate site," such as the forearm (see below).

BLOOD SUGARS SHOULD BE CHECKED:

- four or more times each day (usually before meals and exercise and before bedtime)

- several times each week, approximately two hours after each meal, to assess the adequacy of the meal insulin dose

- anytime the symptoms of a low blood sugar are felt (see Table and Chapter 6)

- occasionally during the night

- anytime unusual symptoms occur (e.g., frequent voiding)

GOALS

The target blood sugars are different for each age group and are shown in the table. At least half of the blood sugar values each time of day should be in the desired range for age. The blood sugar ranges refer both to before meals and at bedtime/overnight.

TABLE: BLOOD SUGAR LEVELS

NON-DIABETIC NORMAL VALUES

70-100 (3.9-5.5)	Normal (fasting)	In mg/dL (mmol/L)
70-140 (3.9-7.8)	Normal (random)*	

PEOPLE WITH DIABETES

Goals	Before Meals Fasting	Bedtime Overnight
Under 6 years	80-180 (4.5-10.0)	130-200 (7.3-11.1)
6-12 years	70-180 (3.9-10.0)	100**-180 (5.5-10.0)
13 years and up	70-150 (3.9-8.3)	90**-150 (5.0-8.3)

Blood/CGM Glucose Levels in mg/dL (mmol/L)		Possible Symptoms
LOW	Below 70 (Below 3.9)	Sweating Hunger Shakiness
"TRUE LOW"	Below 60 (Below 3.3)	Confusion. If not treated, can lead to seizure or unconsciousness episode

Blood/CGM Glucose Levels in mg/dL (mmol/L)		Possible Symptoms
HIGH	200-400 (11.1-22.2)	Low energy Frequent urination
VERY HIGH	400-800 (22.2-44.4)	Stomachache Rapid breathing If not treated, can lead to DKA

*Most values for non-diabetic children are in this range. However, occasional values down to 60 mg/dL (3.3 mmol/L) are still normal.

**If a very heavy exercise day, 130 mg/dL (7.3 mmol/L) might be a better lower level.

ALWAYS BRING YOUR METER (AND LOG BOOK) TO YOUR CLINIC VISITS.

DOING THE BLOOD SUGARS

Finger-Pokes

There are now many good devices. Most can be set for different depths. These may help young children or the elderly who do not need a lancet to go as deep.

How to do the blood sugar

- Get poker ready; insert lancet (change daily).

- Wash hands with soap and warm water; dry. Traces of sugar on the fingertip can greatly raise the value.

- Poke side or tip (not ball) of chosen finger or of arm (alternate site values).

- To get enough blood, hold hand down (below heart level) and "milk" the finger.

- Put the drop of blood on the blood sugar strip as taught for each meter.

- Hold cotton ball on poke site to stop bleeding.

METERS

We do not recommend one meter over another. However, some cheap, low-quality meters are now being sold in stores. If uncertain, check with your diabetes care-provider.

- We like meters that can store at least the last 100 values.

- The meter must also be able to be downloaded by the family or clinic.

- Strips requiring smaller amounts of blood make it easier for young children.

- Make sure the code in the meter matches the code for the strips (if required).

- **The meter must always be brought to the clinic visit.**

The Roche company has developed a meter, the ACCU-CHEK® Aviva Expert, to do the finger stick blood sugar measurement and to then help calculate an insulin bolus dose to give. This insulin dose calculation is similar to what insulin pumps do, but it is for people giving insulin injections. The grams of carbs to be eaten are entered into the meter. Data for insulin to carb ratios and the correction (sensitivity) factor are pre-programmed into the meter for the individual patient for different times of the day. The meter also subtracts active insulin ("insulin on board") from recently administered insulin (if entered into meter). This insulin-dose calculator will be particularly helpful when young children do not have their parents available to determine dose calculations.

ALTERNATE SITE CHECKING

Some meters require such a small drop of blood that it can be obtained from the arm or another site. However, if feeling low, the fingertip must be used as circulation is not as good in other sites and the true blood sugar level may be delayed by 10-20 minutes.

LOG BOOKS

It is important to record results or to download meters at regular intervals.

- Look for patterns of highs and lows.

- If too many lows occur, insulin dose adjustments are needed (e.g., more than two values per week below 60 mg/dL [3.3 mmol/L]). Results can be sent to the nurse or doctor by fax or email if help with insulin dose adjustments is needed.

- If too many highs occur, insulin dose adjustments are needed (e.g., more than two values at the same time of day in a week above 300 mg/dL [16.7 mmol/L]). Results can be sent to the nurse or doctor by fax or email if help with insulin dose adjustments is needed (see Daily Record Sheet on next page).

• We encourage families to learn to make adjustments. If you send blood sugar results, you should suggest solutions to your questions, which can be discussed with a doctor or nurse.

• Parents (even of teens) must do or supervise the recording of the values and the sending of the results.

• **Bring the log book to the clinic visit.**

FEELINGS

It is important not to be upset if highs or lows are found. This can make doing blood sugars a negative experience. Just use the data to adjust the insulin and/or to prevent future highs or lows. We emphasize that sugars are "in target" or "high" or "low," but not "good" or "bad." The only response should be **"Thank you for doing the blood sugar."**

CONTINUOUS GLUCOSE MONITORING (CGM)

Diabetes management is gradually moving toward CGM. This involves wearing a sensor which will send subcutaneous (not blood) glucose values to a receiver. Some blood sugar checking is still necessary. This is now discussed in Chapter 29.

DAILY RECORD SHEET

To Nurse Educator: _____

Patient: _____ Date of Birth: _____ Physician: _____ Parents: _____

Phone: _____ Best time (8am – 5pm) to reach you: _____

Date	Time: / BG/Ket:	Breakfast		Other (optional)		Lunch		Other (optional)		Dinner		Bedtime		Comments (Activity, illness, snacks, etc...)
		Results	Insulin Dose	Results	Insulin Dose	Results	Insulin Dose	Results	Insulin Dose	Results	Insulin Dose	Results	Insulin Dose	
	Time: / BG/Ket:													
	Time: / BG/Ket:													
	Time: / BG/Ket:													
	Time: / BG/Ket:													
	Time: / BG/Ket:													
	Time: / BG/Ket:													
	Time: / BG/Ket:													

Problem Area(s) Noted: _____

Suggested Solution(s): _____

Please note: Make sure insulin doses are included under "Insulin Dose" heading. Copies of this form can be downloaded at http://www.ucdenver.edu/academics/colleges/medicalschool/centers/BarbaraDavis/Clinical/Resources/Pages/healthcare.aspx. Download Word or PDF version of #___. Daily Record Sheet (insulin_daily_rec.doc or insulin_daily_rec.pdf). Or visit, BarbaraDavisCenter.org, Pediatric Clinic, Clinical Resources, Diabetes Resources for Healthcare Providers (#3)...,Daily Record Sheet for Insulin Management (#5 or 6) and choose the injection or pump record sheet.

CHAPTER 8
INSULIN: TYPES AND ACTIVITY

Insulin is a hormone normally made in the islet ('eye-let') cells of the pancreas. It allows sugar to pass into the body's cells to be used for energy (Chapter 2). It is important to understand the type and action of each insulin being used.

WHY ARE INSULIN SHOTS NEEDED?

• Not enough insulin is made in the pancreas of a person with type 1 diabetes.

• Insulin can't be taken as a pill because it would be destroyed by stomach acid.

• People with type 2 diabetes who have ketones or very high blood sugars or HbA1c levels usually take insulin shots, at least in the beginning.

• Some of the insulins discussed below are made available in pre-mixed commercial insulin combinations.

THE FOUR TYPES OF INSULIN ARE:

1) *"rapid-acting/ short lasting"* (Humalog, NovoLog and Apidra) and Regular

   • Humalog, NovoLog and Apidra are more rapid-acting than Regular; they peak earlier and do not last as long as Regular insulin.

   • Humalog, NovoLog, Apidra and Regular insulins are clear.

2) *"intermediate-lasting"* (NPH)

   • NPH insulin is cloudy and must be mixed prior to injecting.

   • The bottles should be turned gently up and down 20 times before drawing the insulin into the syringe.

   • NPH insulin peaks 3-8 hours after being given and lasts 12-15 hours.

3) *"long-lasting"* (Lantus® and Levemir®)

   • These are basal (flat-acting, minimal peak) insulins that last approximately 24 hours.

   • They are clear insulins (don't confuse with rapid-acting insulins).

   • Best given in the bottom (buttocks, seat) to make sure the insulin is given into fat, or into a pinch of fat.

4) *"ultra-long lasting"* (Tresiba® [called Degludec in some countries])

   • A new insulin, Tresiba, has recently been approved in Europe, Japan and Mexico, but not in the U.S.

   • Although used on a daily basis, it lasts for up to three days (72 hours).

   • It has lower day-to-day variability of action and may reduce nighttime low blood sugars.

* Insulin must be stored so that it does not freeze or get over 90° F (32° C) because it will spoil. Otherwise, the insulin vial being used can be kept at room temperature for 30 days.

HOW AND WHEN IS INSULIN USED?

Most people with type 1 diabetes take two or more shots of insulin each day.

RAPID-ACTING INSULIN (HUMALOG, NOVOLOG OR APIDRA)

• Rapid-acting insulins are used to stop the rise of the blood sugar after eating food.

• The rapid-acting insulin (or Regular insulin) can be mixed with NPH insulin to give before breakfast and dinner.

• Most people also take a shot of rapid-acting insulin before lunch and before any snacks (unless taking the snack for low blood sugar).

• Rapid-acting insulin should be taken 20 minutes before the meal. This is because

the peak insulin activity occurs 90 minutes after injection. In contrast, blood sugars peak 60 minutes after food intake (Figure 1). If the blood sugar is below 80 mg/dL (4.5 mmol/L), then take the insulin at meal time.

• If Regular insulin is being used, the shot is usually taken 30-45 minutes before meals.

• For toddlers, the rapid-acting insulin can be given after the meal. Then the dose can be adjusted to fit the amount of food eaten.

• Rapid-acting insulins are also used to "correct" a blood/CGM glucose level that is too high (see Correction Insulin Dose: Chapter 22).

• Regular insulin can be mixed with a rapid-acting insulin to cover high-fat meals (delayed food absorption).

(Reproduced with permission of Diabetes Technology and Therapeutics 12:173, 2010)

Blood sugar levels when insulin was given 20 minutes prior to a meal ("PRE"), at the beginning of the meal ("START"), or after the meal ("POST"). The ADA goal for blood sugars at any time after a meal is not to exceed 180 mg/dL (10 mmol/L).

FIGURE 2

Example of Two Injections Per Day Using a Rapid-Acting Insulin and NPH
H=Humalog, NL=NovoLog, AP= Apidra, R=Regular insulin

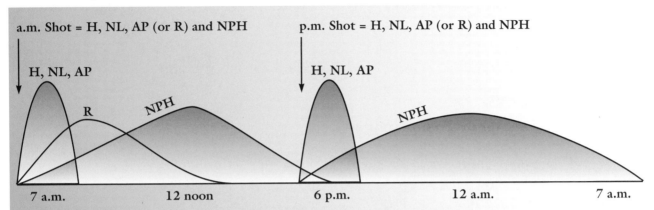

a.m. Shot = H, NL, AP (or R) and NPH   p.m. Shot = H, NL, AP (or R) and NPH

H, NL, AP   R   NPH   H, NL, AP   NPH

7 a.m.   12 noon   6 p.m.   12 a.m.   7 a.m.

Many people receive two injections per day. NPH and a rapid-acting insulin (or Regular) are given prior to breakfast and dinner. When possible, the insulin should be given 20 minutes prior to the meal.

INTERMEDIATE-ACTING INSULIN (NPH)

- NPH insulin has its main effect in 3 to 8 hours and lasts 12 to 15 hours. It is usually taken twice daily in a syringe with a rapid-acting insulin (Figure 2).

- NPH insulin taken at dinner or bedtime has a peak during the night so that low blood sugars are more common compared to when a basal (long-acting) insulin is used.

- People who take three shots per day sometimes take their NPH at bedtime rather than at dinner to help it last through the night. It then has a lesser chance of causing low blood sugars during the night.

LONG-ACTING INSULINS (LANTUS, LEVEMIR OR TRESIBA [Degludec])

Most people using basal-bolus insulin therapy use one of these three insulins for their basal insulin. When using Lantus, Levemir or Tresiba as the basal insulin, the following generally apply (Figures 3-A and 3-B).

- The dose is usually taken alone without any other insulin in the syringe (ask your doctor). Then Humalog, NovoLog or Apidra are taken 20 minutes before each meal (see Figure 3-A).

- Give the insulin into the buttocks (seat) or into a pinch of fat in the stomach (to make sure the insulin is going into the fat).

- The action is very flat and the chance for a low blood sugar is reduced (particularly during the night when the basal insulin is taken in the morning).

- It works as a basal insulin, which prevents the liver from producing sugar. It also prevents the breakdown of fat to release ketones into the blood.

- NPH (an intermediate-acting insulin) is sometimes also taken in the morning, particularly if a noon shot cannot be taken (Figure 3-B). It can be given in the same syringe with the rapid-acting insulin.

- The dose is judged on the basis of the morning blood sugar no matter when the Lantus, Levemir or Tresiba shot is taken (a.m., lunch, dinner or bedtime; all times work – though one consistent time must be chosen). If the blood sugar is consistently above the desired range (Chapter 7) at breakfast, the dose is increased. If below the lower level, the dose is decreased.

- Often Levermir (or Lantus) is given twice a day if it does not seem to last for 24 hours.

Two of the most common methods of using Lantus, Levemir or Tresiba insulin:

FIGURE 3-A

Use of Lantus, Levemir or Tresiba Insulin

In the first example, Lantus, Levemir or Tresiba is used as the basal insulin (given in the a.m., or at dinner or at bedtime) and a rapid-acting insulin is taken 20 minutes prior to meals and snacks. This is often referred to as basal-bolus insulin therapy.

FIGURE 3-B

In this second example, NPH and a rapid-acting insulin are taken in one syringe 20 minutes prior to breakfast. A rapid-acting insulin is taken alone 20 minutes prior to dinner. Lantus, Levemir or Tresiba (alone in the syringe) is taken consistently either in the a.m., at dinner, or at bedtime.

CHAPTER 9
DRAWING UP INSULIN AND GIVING INSULIN INJECTIONS

The nurse-educator will teach the best way to draw up and to give the insulin. Both are described in this chapter. A section on the use of insulin pens is also included below. Finally, a summary of giving shots to children of different ages is provided.

DRAWING UP INSULIN (Figure 1)

A. Get everything you will need:

- a bottle of each insulin you will use

- syringe

- alcohol wipe for tops of bottles

- log book with current blood sugar results and insulin dose. Please record each blood sugar result and insulin dose in log book.

B. How to draw insulin into the syringe (example of drawing two insulins into a syringe)

- Know how much of each insulin you need to give (based on "thinking" scales if appropriate – see Chapter 22 in "*Understanding Diabetes*"). Eventually the dose will also be based on carbohydrate counting (Chapter 12) and a correction factor (Chapter 22).

- Wipe off the tops of insulin bottles with alcohol swab.

- Inject air into the intermediate-acting (cloudy) insulin bottle with the bottle sitting upright on the table and remove the needle.*

- Inject air in the clear (rapid-acting) insulin bottle and leave the needle in the bottle.*

- Turn the rapid-acting bottle with the needle in it upside down and draw approximately 5 units of insulin in and out of the syringe to get rid of any air bubbles. (See this chapter in "*Understanding Diabetes*" for specific steps that can be used to get rid of air bubbles.) Draw up the clear rapid-acting insulin you need and remove the needle from the bottle. (Note- if drawing up only one insulin, you have now completed the task.)

- Mix the cloudy (NPH) insulin by gently turning the bottle up and down 20 times; this mixes the insulin so that it will have a consistent strength.

- Turn the bottle upside down and put the needle into the bottle. Draw up the cloudy insulin into the syringe. *Make sure not to push any rapid-acting insulin already in the syringe back into this bottle.*

- If the insulin bottles have been in the refrigerator, you can warm up the insulin once it is mixed in the syringe by holding the syringe in the closed palm of your hand for a minute. It will be less likely to sting if the insulin is at room temperature.

*An option now used by some people is to not put air into the insulin bottles, but to just "vent" the bottles once a week to remove any vacuum. This is done by removing the plunger from the syringe and inserting the needle into the upright insulin bottle. Air will be sucked in through the needle removing the vacuum from the bottle. (The vacuum may otherwise pull insulin from the syringe into the insulin bottle. This is most important if two insulins are being mixed in the same syringe.)

GIVING THE INSULIN

- Choose the area of the body where you are going to give the shot. Use four or more areas and use different sites within the area (see Figure 2).

- Make sure the area where you will be giving the shot is clean.

- Relax the chosen area (see "Different Age Children" section below for techniques).

- Pull up the skin with the finger and thumb (even with short needles).

- Touch the needle to the skin and "punch" it through the skin.

If Short Needle:
a 90° angle for the 5/16 inch (short) or the BD Ultra-Fine Nano needle (these hurt less and are not as likely to go into muscle)(a 90° angle looks like this: _↓_)

If Longer Needle:
use a 45° angle for the 5/8 inch needle (only)(a 45° angle looks like this: _↘_)

- Push in the insulin slowly and steadily; wait 10 seconds to let the insulin spread out.

- Let go of the skin pulled up.

- Put a finger or dry cotton over the needle as it is pulled out; gently rub a few times to close the hole where the needle was inserted; press your finger or the cotton down on the area where you gave the shot if bruising or bleeding happens.

- Look to see if a drop of insulin comes back through the hole the needle made ("leak-back"); make a note in your log book if this happens.

The nurse will teach the right way to give shots so that a drop of insulin does not leak-back. A drop can contain as much as five units of insulin.

FIGURE 1

DRAWING AND INJECTING THE INSULIN

A. Wash hands

B. Warm and mix (if NPH) insulin

C. Wipe top of insulin bottle with alcohol

D. Inject air = insulin dose in units

   Pull out dose of insulin

E. Make sure injection site is clean

F. Pinch up skin and fat tissue. If using 5/8 inch needle, go in at angle. If using the 5/16 inch (short) or the BD Ultra-Fine Nano needle, can go straight in (assuming adequate subcutaneous fat).

G. Basal insulins (Lantus, Levemir and Tresiba) are best given in the buttocks

INSULIN PENS

Insulin pens provide convenience and accuracy. Most types of insulin are now available in pens. Using a pen is quite easy and is summarized below.

- Remove the paper tab from the needle and screw it on the end of the pen.

- Clean the skin where the shot will be given. Rotate sites daily.

- Remove the needle cover.

- Enter 2 to 3 units (by rotating the dial) in the pen as a "priming dose" and with the needle pointed upward into the air, push in plunger and observe that the insulin comes out.

- Dial in the number of units to be given.

- Insert the needle under the skin.

- Inject the insulin slowly. Then count 10 seconds before removing the needle. (This prevents insulin from leaking out.)

- Rub the injection site gently to close the track of the needle.

- Put the cover back on the needle. Some say to change the needle with each injection and others say once daily.

DIFFERENT AGE CHILDREN AND INSULIN SHOTS

- A young child can help with choosing where the shot will be given (although sites must be rotated) and by holding still.

- Children usually begin to give some of their own shots around age 10.

- It is important that both mom and dad share in giving shots.

- Some age-related issues (see Chapter 18) are summarized below.

Toddlers

- This age group can sometimes be frightened when having to get shots.

- Keep the area where the shot will be given as still as possible. Try to get the child's attention on something else (e.g., television, blowing bubbles, looking at a book, etc.). This will help the child to relax.

- The buttocks are often used first, and later the legs and arms and tummy.

- With the child's permission, the Lantus, Levemir or Tresiba insulin can be given when the child is asleep.

- The parent must remember when giving their child a shot, they are giving them health.

School age

- The child may help in choosing the area on their body to give the shot.

- Change where the shots are given. Use two or more areas (e.g., abdomen and bottom) and use different sites within the areas (see Figure 2).

Teens

- Many teens give their own shots and do not want help.

- It is still important to give the shots in a place (e.g., the kitchen) where parents can actually see the shot given.

- Missing shots (boluses) is a common reason for poor blood sugar control.

- Parents can stay involved by helping to get the supplies out, and helping to keep records by writing down the blood sugars and insulin doses each day in the log book or by emailing meter or CGM downloads.

FIGURE 2

Commonly used injection sites are numbered. Rotating between sites is important to prevent swelling (hypertrophy) and altered insulin absorption.

Chapter 10 – Feelings/Adjustments at Diabetes Onset

CHAPTER 10
FEELINGS/ADJUSTMENT AT DIABETES ONSET

INTIAL FEELINGS

You and your child will have many feelings when you find out about diabetes. Having these feelings is very normal. It is important for families to share and talk about these feelings.

Some of the most common feelings are:

- **shock**

- **grief**

- **denial**

- **sadness**

- **anger**

- **fear/anxiety**

- **guilt**

- **adapting (as time passes, everyone will not feel so overwhelmed)**

These emotions are normal during the initial diagnosis period. Each of these feelings is discussed in detail in the larger book, *"Understanding Diabetes"* (order form in back).

We ask **EVERY** newly diagnosed family to meet with a behavioral counselor to discuss feelings. The person may be a social worker, licensed professional counselor, psychologist (a PhD), or a psychiatrist (an MD). It is important for all family members to share how they feel. All family members need to work together to learn how to fit diabetes into their lives.

As time passes, the family will find they are better able to deal with the shots, blood sugar checks, food plan and other daily tasks. Parents need to learn to share responsibilities.

ADJUSTMENT

Making life with diabetes as normal as possible is the major long-term goal. Living with diabetes will gradually become easier. Adjustment continues to improve after the first few weeks and the first few months. As time passes, the tasks below will become easier:

- exercising daily

- selecting healthy food choices

- adjusting insulin for exercise

- remembering to take insulin and/or other medications

- checking blood sugar levels

- counting carbohydrates

- doing other daily diabetes related tasks

Talking about diabetes at home and/or with the diabetes care team may help to reduce stress and create a comfortable schedule. Fitting the diabetes into as normal a lifestyle as possible becomes the major goal.

The period around initial diagnosis can be filled with many different feelings. These are normal, and tend to improve over time. Some families have recurrence of these feelings at specific times in their child's life. This will be discussed in Chapter 17.

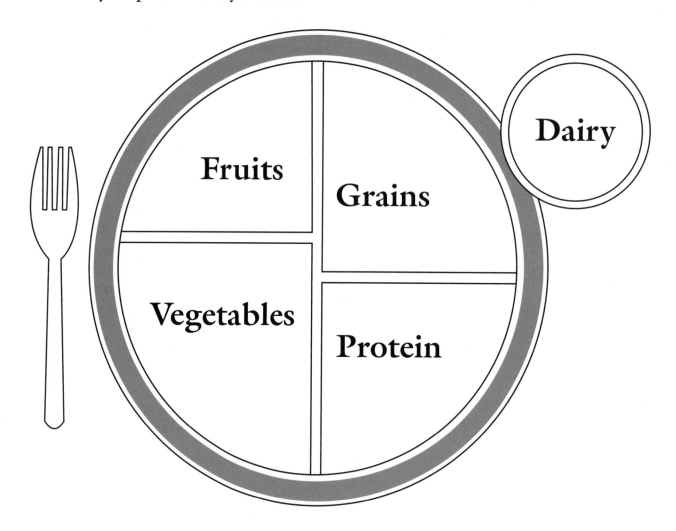

Choose**MyPlate**.gov
(a helpful website)

Look at the food plate guide to see if you need to:

• eat more whole-grain foods (e.g., whole wheat bread, brown rice, cereals)

• eat more fruits and vegetables

• eat less protein and fat (particularly red meat)

Some knowledge of normal nutrition helps when working with the dietitian on a diabetes food plan. Energy from food is measured in calories.

TYPES OF FOODS

The foods we eat are divided into:

- **proteins – 4 calories per gram eaten**

- **carbohydrates (includes all sugars: 4 calories per gram eaten)**

- **fats – 9 calories per gram eaten**

- **vitamins and minerals**

- **water**

- **fiber**

All of these are important for our bodies and are discussed in more detail in *"Understanding Diabetes."* We emphasize with patients and families that the ideal diet for someone with diabetes is really just a healthy diet from which all people would benefit.

WEIGHT MANAGEMENT

Some people with type 2 diabetes can be treated with diet and exercise alone. This is not true for type 1 diabetes. In recent years, people with type 1 diabetes have also tended to be heavier. This results in more insulin resistance and a higher risk for heart disease. This is why snacks are no longer routinely recommended (unless on NPH insulin). **Reduction of high fat foods** and **portion control** (along with **exercise**) are important for everyone.

Foods higher in fat include:

- red meats

- the skin of chicken or turkey

- whole milk

- fats and oils

- processed foods

- fast foods

INSULIN AND CARBOHYDRATES (CARBS)

Insulin has its main effect on sugars and a goal of treatment is matching insulin to carbohydrate intake. **It is important to think about the following:**

- **WHEN** carbohydrate is eaten.

  Snacks between meals makes blood sugar control more challenging.

- **HOW MUCH** carbohydrate is eaten. A can of sugar pop has 10 teaspoons of sugar and is unhealthy for anyone.

- **WITH WHAT** the carbohydrate is eaten. Other foods, such as fat, slow the sugar absorption.

- **IF INSULIN IS ACTING** at the same time the sugar is eaten. This allows the sugar to pass into cells for energy rather than out into the urine (see Chapter 2).

THE "PLATE" METHOD OF CHOOSING FOOD

A U.S. Department of Agriculture Center has provided an easy-to-understand guide for foods to eat. They suggest one quarter of your plate has the following food groups:

- lean protein
- fruits
- vegetables
- whole-grain carbohydrate foods

Low-fat dairy products can be added (see Figure on page 42)

EATING NUTRITIOUS FOODS WILL HELP ALL FAMILY MEMBERS.

OTHER THOUGHTS discussed in Chapter 11 of *"Understanding Diabetes"* are noted below:

- Working with the dietitian helps families keep up-to-date on new dietary ideas.

- A three-day diet record is sometimes helpful.

- Learning to read nutrition labels on foods at the store is very important.

- Having normal levels of blood fats (e.g., total cholesterol and LDL cholesterol) is important for all people. These levels can be checked once yearly at a clinic visit. See Table in Chapter 23 for desired levels.

- Sugar-containing drinks such as soda are a source of "empty calories" and are unhealthy for all. They contribute to obesity and cause high blood sugar levels in people with diabetes.

CHAPTER 12
FOOD MANAGEMENT AND DIABETES

A food plan is important for people with either type 1 or type 2 diabetes. Every family must work out a plan with their dietitian that fits their family. As shown in the diagram in Chapter 14, food and exercise are two of the four major influences on sugar control. Both are important if excess weight is present or is to be avoided.

People with type 1 diabetes cannot be treated with diet alone.

People with type 2 diabetes can sometimes be treated with diet and exercise alone. They generally need to eat foods with fewer calories and choose smaller portion sizes to attain optimal weight.

All people with diabetes should focus on a healthy, balanced diet (see Chapter 12 in *"Understanding Diabetes"*) and need to:

- avoid concentrated sweets (such as sugar pop)
- reduce fat content in their diet
- avoid unhealthy choices at fast food restaurants (burger, fries, pizza)
- eat more fruits and vegetables
- exercise at least 60 minutes daily

TYPES OF FOOD PLANS

The two types of food plans that our Clinic uses the most are outlined below. Both plans require learning how to count (or estimate) carbohydrates (which are the main food source increasing blood sugar levels).

Constant carbohydrate: A person/family often starts with this plan.

- This plan involves eating about the same amount of carbs for each meal and for each snack from day to day.
- Insulin doses are changed based on the blood sugar levels, exercise, and other factors such as illness, stress, menses, etc. ("thinking scale").

Carbohydrate ("carb") counting: We encourage families to move to this plan as soon as possible. The plan involves counting the grams of carbohydrate (carbs) in food to be eaten. An amount of rapid-acting insulin is given that matches the number of grams (g) of carbohydrate (I/C ratio = insulin to carb ratio). Other parameters relating to starting carb counting are outlined below.

- The dietitian may want a three-day diet record to be done first (see Chapter 11 in *"Understanding Diabetes"*).
- The healthcare team and family initially determine the insulin-to-carb ratio (I/C ratio) for each time of day.
- The ratio used when starting this plan depends on the patient. A common starting example is one unit of insulin for each 15g of carbohydrate (I/C ratio of 1 to 15).
- Blood/CGM glucose levels are then evaluated 2 to 4 hours after meals to see if the I/C ratio of 1 to 15 is correct.

- If the blood sugar level is high two-hours after eating (e.g., over 180 mg/dL or 10.0 mmol/L), the ratio could be changed to one unit of insulin for 10g of carbs (I/C ratio of 1 to 10).

- If the blood sugar level is low two hours after eating (e.g., less than 60 mg/dL or 3.3 mmol/L), the ratio could be changed to one unit of insulin for 20g of carbs (I/C ratio of 1 to 20).

- Gradually, the correct ratios for each meal are found. The I/C ratio may vary for each meal.

- A blood sugar level is measured and an insulin dose "correction factor" (see Chapter 22) is used to adjust the dose. The insulin for food (I/C ratio) plus the correction dose will be the total dose of insulin to be given 20 minutes before the meal or snack.

- If blood sugar levels are above the desired upper level one or two hours after meals (and the pre-meal blood sugar level is above 80 mg/dL [4.5 mmol/L]), it may be helpful to give the pre-meal rapid-acting insulin 20 minutes before meals. This is because blood sugar levels peak in 60 minutes after a meal, whereas Humalog/NovoLog/Apidra insulins do not peak until 90 minutes after injection.

Several tables of the carb contents of foods and more details about carb counting are found in Chapter 12 of the book *"Understanding Diabetes."*

BEDTIME SNACKS

People often ask if bedtime snacks are needed. If a person has had heavy exercise, or if the blood sugar level is below 130 mg/dL (7.3 mmol/L), or if a peaking insulin (e.g., NPH) is taken at night, then make sure a bedtime snack that has solid protein, fat and carbohydrate is eaten. Otherwise, if a basal insulin is used, and the blood sugar level

is above 130 mg/dL (>7.3 mmol/L) and there has not been heavy exercise, a bedtime snack may not be required as it can lead to unhealthy weight gain.

HELPFUL SUGGESTIONS FOR FOOD MANAGEMENT

Some beginning suggestions for food management, some of which relate more to a constant carb food plan, are:

- avoid concentrated sweets

- eat well-balanced meals

- eat meals and snacks at approximately the same time each day

- watch the portion size of foods to be eaten

- snacks may be needed to prevent insulin reactions, especially with exercise (see suggested snacks in Chapter 12 of *"Understanding Diabetes"*). Reducing insulin as needed for exercise rather than eating extra snacks will be better for weight control.

- avoid over-treating low blood sugars

- eat foods with less cholesterol, saturated fats and trans-fats

- reduce total fat intake

- monitor for appropriate growth

- watch weight for height; avoid becoming overweight

- increase the amount of fiber eaten

- eat fewer foods that are high in salt (sodium)

- avoid eating too much protein

- complete dietary guidelines are available at www.dietaryguidelines.gov

TABLE

Six Dietary Factors to Aid with Sugar Control*

1. Following some sort of a meal plan	4. Not eating extra snacks
2. Not over-treating low blood sugars (hypoglycemia)	5. Prompt treatment of high blood sugars when found
3. Adjusting insulin levels for meals	6. Consistency of bedtime snacks

* from the **DCCT**: Diabetes Control and Complications Trial (see Chapter 14)

GETTING PLENTY OF EXERCISE IS IMPORTANT FOR EVERYONE.

CHAPTER 13
EXERCISE AND DIABETES

Regular exercise is important for everyone. It may be even more important for people with diabetes. For people with type 2 diabetes, regular exercise and eating less food are two of the most important parts of treating the diabetes (see Chapter 4). Many former and present professional athletes have diabetes (see "*Understanding Diabetes,*" Chapter 13).

These athletes do not let diabetes get in the way of their careers.

Exercise may lower or raise (due to adrenaline output) the blood sugar levels. Overall, exercise helps to keep the blood sugar values in the target range. It does this in part by making us more sensitive to insulin.

FIGURE

Blood Sugars With and Without One Hour of Exercise

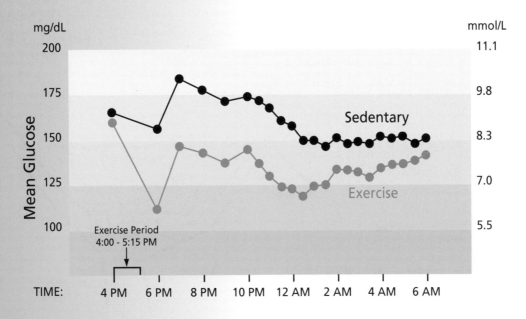

This Figure presents blood glucose (sugar) levels for the same 50 children with type 1 diabetes on a sedentary day (black circles) and an exercise day (red circles). The one hour of exercise at 4 p.m. resulted in lower blood sugar levels for the next 14 hours (through the night). Insulin doses and food intake were identical for the two days.

(Data compliments of the DirecNet Study Group: J Pediatr 147, 528, 2005)

EXERCISE:

- is one of the "big four," along with insulin or oral medicines, food and stress, which affects blood sugar levels (see Figure 2 in Chapter 14)

- is essential for weight control and is a primary part of treating type 2 diabetes

- should be done daily for 60 minutes by people with type 1 or type 2 diabetes (and by all people)

- generally lowers blood sugar levels (see Figure)

- requires extra fluids during exercise to prevent dehydration

PREVENTING LOWS

Exercise can cause **low blood sugar values** (Chapter 6) so it is important to plan ahead. If a low blood sugar does occur, it is important to stop the exercise, treat the low blood sugar, and not resume exercise until the blood sugar level is back up. The following may help to prevent lows:

- extra snacks or less insulin may be needed. When possible, reduce insulin for exercise instead of increasing snacks. This will help lead to a healthier weight.

- aiming for a higher blood sugar level before exercise (e.g., 180 mg/dL [10.0 mmol/L])

- use of drinks (such as Gatorade®) during vigorous exercise

- thinking ahead to prevent low blood sugars for up to 24 hours after the exercise ("delayed hypoglycemia") such as:

  ◊ the evening insulin dose may need to be reduced

  ◊ adding an extra 15 or 30 grams of carbohydrate at bedtime if afternoon or evening exercise has been strenuous without taking extra insulin

  ◊ making sure the bedtime blood/CGM glucose value is above 130 mg/dL (7.3 mmol/L)

- doing extra blood sugar levels

INSULIN PUMPS

- Use of an insulin pump and/or CGM makes insulin adjustments easier to prevent exercise-related hypoglycemia.

- Using reduced temporary basal rates during and after exercise can be helpful (Chapter 28).

- Some insulin-pump users who disconnect from their pump during exercise can benefit by giving part of their basal insulin as Lantus, Levemir or Tresiba (Degludec) and part via the pump. For example, half of the basal insulin could be given by the pump (50% temp basal for 24 hours) and the other half given as a shot of one of the above basal insulins.

EXERCISE CAN BE FUN . . .

. . . AND WET!

LEARN TO BALANCE FOOD, INSULIN (OR ORAL MEDICINES), STRESS, AND EXERCISE FOR OPTIMAL SUGAR CONTROL.

CHAPTER 14
MONITORING DIABETES CONTROL

A goal for the management of diabetes is to have blood sugar levels as close to the levels of someone without diabetes as is safely possible. At least half of all values should be "in-range" for age (see Table 1).

SUGAR* CONTROL

• is measured day to day by checking blood sugar levels on a meter or, more recently, by a continuous glucose monitor (CGM) (see Chapter 29)

• is monitored for the longer term by a very important measurement called the hemoglobin A1c (**HbA1c or A1c; see Figure 1**)

THE HbA1c (A1c) VALUE

• can be thought of as the **"forest"** and the blood/CGM** sugar values as the **"trees"**

• increases when blood sugars are high (see Figure 1)

• tells how often the sugars have been high for every second of the day for the past 90 days

• should be done every three months

• should be in the desired age range (see Table 1) for a person to be in "optimal sugar control." Others (ISPAD) have suggested not using an "age range" for the desired HbA1c levels, and to just have a goal of below 7.5% (< 58 mmol/mol) for all children.

The best goal is to have an HbA1c as low as possible (no lower than 6.0% [42 mmol/mol]), balanced with infrequent hypoglycemia and a high quality of life. Having an HbA1c too low may result in excessive hypoglycemia.

BLOOD/ CGM SUGAR LEVELS**

• Ranges for blood/CGM sugar values should be set for every person (see Table 1).

• Meters and CGMs can usually be downloaded to a computer to provide the percent of values in-range, high and low. This data should be reviewed at least weekly. Aim for over 50 percent of values in-range and no more than 10 percent low.

• Meters and CGMs can usually display 7, 14 or 30 day averages. These can be used to know if dose changes are working or more changes are needed.

• Blood sugar control has four major influences (Figure 2).

WHY IS SUGAR CONTROL IMPORTANT?

Optimal sugar control:

• helps people feel better

• can lessen the future risk for eye, kidney, nerve and heart problems from diabetes. This was proven by The **DCCT** (**D**iabetes **C**ontrol and **C**omplications **T**rial)

* In this book, the words "sugar" and "glucose" are used to have the same meaning.
** When the term "blood/CGM" is used, it indicates the sugar may have been measured from a blood sample or by a continuous glucose monitor (CGM).

- helps to lower blood fats (cholesterol and triglyceride levels; see Chapter 11)
- includes reduction of the wide "swings" (variability) in blood/CGM sugar levels
- helps children grow to their full adult height
- reduces the risks for diabetic ketoacidosis (DKA; Chapter 15) and severe hypoglycemia (see Chapter 6)
- is a reflection of the balancing of food, insulin (or oral meds), exercise and stress (see Figure 2)

We believe that a lower HbA1c is better, but this must be balanced with a good quality of life and infrequent hypoglycemia.

YOU CAN DO IT!

TABLE 1

Recommended HbA1c and Blood Glucose (Sugar) Values		
	Hemoglobin A1c	Blood Glucose: mg/dL (mmol/L)**
	HbA1c: % (mmol/mol)**	Fasting/Before Meals* / 2 Hours Post-meal Bedtime/Overnight*
Normal (Non-Diabetic)	<6.0% (<42)	70-100 (3.9-5.5)* / 70-140 (3.9-7.8)
Borderline Levels	5.7-6.4% (39-46)	100-125 (5.5-6.9) / 140-200 (7.8-11.1)
Diabetes	>6.4% (>46)	>125 (6.9) / >200 (11.1)
Desired ranges for someone with diabetes:		
0-6 years	<7.5% (<58)***	80-180 (4.5-10.0) / 130-200 (7.3-11.1)
6-12 years	<7.5% (<58)***	70-180 (3.9-10.0) / 100-180 (5.5-10.0)
13-19 years	<7.5% (<58)	70-150 (3.9-8.3) / 90-150 (5.0-8.3)
>19 years	<7.0% (<53)	70-130 (3.9-7.3) / 70-140 (3.9-7.8)

< =less than; > =greater than

*Values for fasting and 2 hours as in the oral glucose tolerance test (OGTT).

**Values in parentheses represent mmol/L (glucose) or mmol/mol (HbA1c). The HbA1c levels are as recommended by the ADA in 2014.

***ISPAD also recommends HbA1c levels of <7.5% (58mmol/mol) for all ages of children.

FIGURE 1

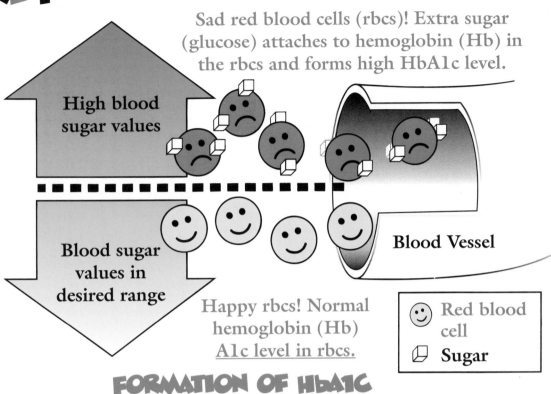

Sad red blood cells (rbcs)! Extra sugar (glucose) attaches to hemoglobin (Hb) in the rbcs and forms high HbA1c level.

High blood sugar values

Blood sugar values in desired range

Blood Vessel

Happy rbcs! Normal hemoglobin (Hb) A1c level in rbcs.

Red blood cell

Sugar

FORMATION OF HbA1C

FIGURE 2

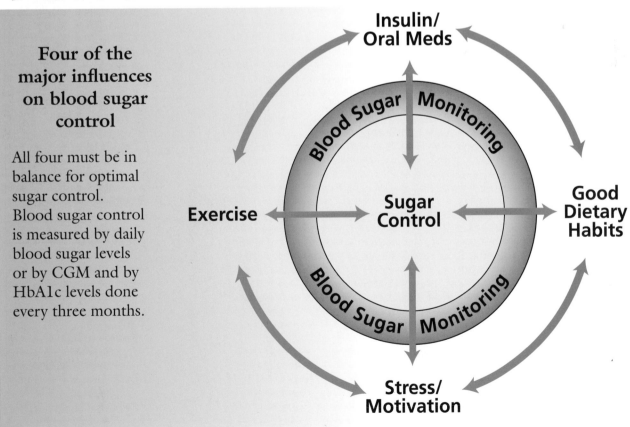

Four of the major influences on blood sugar control

All four must be in balance for optimal sugar control. Blood sugar control is measured by daily blood sugar levels or by CGM and by HbA1c levels done every three months.

Insulin/ Oral Meds

Blood Sugar Monitoring

Exercise

Sugar Control

Good Dietary Habits

Blood Sugar Monitoring

Stress/ Motivation

Comparison of the Two Emergencies of Diabetes

	Low Blood Sugar (B.S.) (Chapter 6) (Hypoglycemia or Insulin Reaction)	Ketoacidosis (Chapter 15) (Acidosis or DKA)
Due to:	Low blood sugar (B.S.)	Presence of ketones
Time of onset:	Fast – within minutes	Slow – in hours or days
Causes:	Too little food Too much insulin Too much exercise without food Missing or being late for meals/snacks Excitement in young children	Too little insulin Not giving insulin Infections/Illness Traumatic body stress Pump insertions malfunctioning
Blood sugar:	Low (below 70 mg/dL or 3.9 mmol/L)	Usually high (over 240 mg/dL or 13.3 mmol/L)
Ketones:	Usually none in the urine or blood	Usually moderate/large in the urine or blood ketones over 0.6 mmol/L
	SYMPTOMS	**SYMPTOMS**
Mild:	Hunger, shaky, sweaty, nervous	Thirst, frequent urination, sweet breath, small or moderate urine ketones or blood ketones less than 1.0 mmol/L
Moderate:	Headache, unexpected behavior changes, impaired or double vision, confusion, drowsiness, weakness or difficulty talking.	Dry mouth, nausea, stomach cramps, vomiting, moderate or large urine ketones or blood ketones between 1.0 and 3.0 mmol/L
Severe:	Loss of consciousness or seizures occurs after being low for a prolonged time.	Labored deep breathing, extreme weakness, confusion and eventually unconsciousness (coma): large urine ketones or blood ketones above 3.0 mmol/L.
	TREATMENT	**TREATMENT**
Mild:	Give juice or milk. Wait 15 minutes and recheck B.S. Repeat as needed	Give lots of fluids and Humalog/NovoLog/Aprida or Regular insulin every two or three hours.
Moderate:	Give instant glucose or a fast-acting sugar, juice or sugar pop (4 oz). After 15 minutes, recheck B.S. Repeat as needed	Continued contact with healthcare provider. Give lots of fluids. Give Humalog/NovoLog/Aprida or Regular insulin every two hours. Give Zofran (a tablet) or Phenergan medication (suppository or topical cream) if vomiting occurs.
Severe:	Give glucagon into muscle or fat. Check blood sugar. If no response, call paramedic (911) or go to E.R.	*Go to the emergency room.* May need intravenous fluids and insulin.

56   Chapter 15 – Ketones and Diabetic KetoAcidosis (DKA)

CHAPTER 15
KETONES AND DIABETIC KETOACIDOSIS (DKA)

This is the second emergency for people with diabetes (the other being low blood sugar; Chapter 6). DKA is more common in people with type 1 compared to type 2 diabetes, but can occur in type 2 diabetes. Low blood sugar is more common than DKA, although episodes of DKA are more dangerous. DKA is generally easy to differentiate from low blood sugar (see Table).

WHAT LEADS TO DKA?

DKA occurs when ketones build up in the body because there isn't enough insulin. DKA is avoidable in a person with known diabetes.

Ketones are:

• made by the body from breaking down fat when there is not enough insulin in the body and sugar cannot be used for energy

• an acid that forms when the body uses fat for the energy it needs

HOW DOES IT START?

• The body makes ketones when there isn't enough insulin. Ketones can be measured in the urine or blood (see Chapter 5).

• The longer the body doesn't get the insulin it needs, the higher the ketone (acid) level. Excess ketones result in **DKA** (**D**iabetic **K**eto**A**cidosis).

WHAT ARE THE MAIN CAUSES OF INCREASED KETONES OR OF DKA?

• Forgetting to give one or more insulin shots is the most common cause of DKA in patients with known diabetes.

• Illness: the amount of insulin usually needs to be increased from the person's normal doses so the body will have the extra energy from carbohydrates needed to fight the illness. Otherwise, fat is broken down to provide energy and ketones rise. This is why we recommend checking ketones with all illnesses.

• Not enough insulin (dose too small) may result in ketone build-up.

• An insulin pump that is not delivering insulin (usually due to kinked, obstructed or dislodged infusion catheter) may result in ketones in three hours.

• Giving "spoiled" insulin (insulin that got too hot [over 90° F, 32° C] or froze) can be a cause of increased ketones.

• Traumatic stress on the body (particularly for people with type 2 diabetes) may cause ketones.

DKA can be very dangerous. It usually does not occur unless large urine ketones or high blood ketones (above 3.0 mmol/L) have been present for several hours. See the Table for advice on treatment of different levels of ketones. It can be avoided in people with known diabetes by checking blood or urine ketones as instructed (see following).

WHAT ARE THE SIGNS OF DKA?

- Thirst and frequent urination are common due to the associated high blood sugar levels.

- A stomachache, vomiting, or a sweet or fruity odor to the breath (like acetone, or nail polish remover) can occur with high ketones.

- If large urine ketones or blood ketones above 3.0 mmol/L have been present for many hours, deep or rapid breathing can occur. This is a late sign of DKA. You need to go to the emergency room immediately!

WHEN SHOULD KETONES BE CHECKED?

Check for blood or urine ketones (see methods in Chapter 5):

- with any illness (even vomiting one time)

- anytime two or more blood sugar levels are above 300 mg/dL (16.7 mmol/L) at any time during the day

- anytime the first morning blood/CGM glucose level is above 300 mg/dL (16.7 mmol/L)

- with a pump infusion set failure

- when a basal insulin shot has been missed

TREATMENT OF ELEVATED KETONES

- It is important to drink extra liquids. The extra liquids help to wash out the ketones and prevent dehydration.

- When ketones are high, it is best to **NOT** exercise as the ketone level may increase.

- It is important to keep the blood sugar level up (e.g., above 100 mg/dL [5.5 mmol/L]) so that enough insulin can be given to turn off ketone production without having low blood sugar (see Chapter 16 on Sick Day Management).

- If help is needed, call the diabetes care-provider when moderate or large urine ketones are found, or if the blood ketones are above 1.0 mmol/L.

- Extra doses of rapid-acting insulin (by shot if using an insulin pump) will be needed every two hours until the high blood ketones or the moderate or large urine ketones are gone. The family can make repeat calls every two hours to the doctor or nurse if help is needed.

- If trouble breathing or vomiting more than three times occurs, you need to go to the Emergency Department.

We have found that DKA can be prevented 95 percent of the time in a person with known diabetes if the instructions in this chapter are followed.

DRINKING FLUIDS HELPS REMOVE KETONES FROM THE BODY.

REMEMBER TO CHECK FOR KETONES!

HIGH BLOOD SUGAR LEVELS WILL MAKE YOU GO THE BATHROOM MORE OFTEN, RESULTING IN AN INCREASE IN THIRST.

CHECK YOUR KETONES
BEFORE CALLING YOUR DOCTOR
WHEN YOU AREN'T FEELING WELL.

CHAPTER 16
SICK DAY/SURGERY MANAGEMENT

SICK DAY MANAGEMENT

People with diabetes get sick just like other people. For example, the average child gets six to eight colds a year. These may affect the diabetes. More frequent blood sugar checking and/or use of the continuous glucose monitor (CGM) can be very helpful during times of illness.

Ketones

- Always check **urine and/or blood ketones** (see Chapter 5) and the **blood/CGM glucose levels** with any illness. Check ketones even if the blood sugar level is normal.

- The earlier you treat the ketones with extra Humalog/NovoLog/Apidra (or Regular) insulin and fluids, the less chance you will have to go into the hospital. Repeat injections (by shot if using an insulin pump) are given every two hours until the ketones are below moderate in the urine or below 0.6 mmol/L in the blood.

- Call your diabetes doctor or nurse if the urine ketone result is moderate or large or if the blood ketone level is above 1.0 mmol/L and you need assistance (see Chapter 15 on prevention of DKA).

Insulin

- If vomiting is present and ketones are negative, the insulin dose may have to be lowered, but **some insulin must still be given.** Ketones usually start to form after three hours without insulin, but may appear in less time when sick.

- If the person vomits three or more times, some doctors will prescribe a Phenergan suppository (or skin-application) or orally dissolved tablets called Zofran®. Children under two years of age should not use a Phenergan suppository. Phenergan and Zofran cause drowsiness. For this reason, the person will need assistance to make sure blood sugar or urine ketones are checked every 2-3 hours if these medications are used. Some doctors do not prescribe these medications due to concerns of missing DKA. Other information related to handling vomiting is given in Table 1.

Low-Dose Glucagon

- A low-dose may be helpful when the blood sugar is low and vomiting continues (see Chapter 6).

- Glucagon can be mixed and given with an insulin syringe just like insulin.

- The dose of glucagon is much lower than the dose given for severe hypoglycemia.

- The dose is one unit for every year of age up to 15 units.

- It should <u>not</u> be given if urine ketones are moderate or large (or blood ketones above 1.0 mmol/L).

- The glucagon can be repeated every 20 minutes if needed.

Other Medications/Foods/Care

Many medications have a warning label that a person with diabetes should not use the medicine. This is often because they may raise the blood/CGM glucose levels a few points.

Management of vomiting (without ketones)

- Avoid solid foods until the vomiting has stopped.

- If vomiting is frequent, some doctors recommend giving a Phenergan suppository (or skin application) or an orally dissolved tablet called Zofran to reduce vomiting. It may be best to wait to give fluids for an hour until the medicine is working. Children under two years of age should not use a Phenergan suppository. If you use these medications, the blood sugar and ketone monitoring directions must be followed (see text).

- Gradually start liquids (juice, Pedialyte®, water, etc.) in small amounts. Juices (especially orange) replace the salts that are lost with vomiting or diarrhea. Pedialyte popsicles are also available.

- Start with a tablespoon of liquid every 10-20 minutes.

- If the blood/CGM glucose level is below 100 mg/dL (5.5 mmol/L) sugar pop or other liquids containing sugar can be given.

- If the blood sugar level is below 70 mg/dL (3.9 mmol/L) and the person is vomiting, give a low-dose of glucagon just as you would give insulin. The dose is 1 unit per year of age up to 15 units (see text). Repeat doses can be given every 20 minutes as needed.

- If the blood sugar level is above 150 mg/dL (8.3 mmol/L), do not give pop or other drink with sugar in it.

- If there is no further vomiting, gradually increase the amount of fluid.

- If vomiting restarts, it may again be necessary to rest the stomach for another hour and then restart the small amounts of fluids. A repeat Phenergan suppository or Zofran tablet can be given after three or four hours.

- After a few hours without vomiting, gradually return to a normal diet. Soups are often helpful to start with and they provide needed nutrients.

- If this is the case, go ahead and take it. The insulin dose can be adjusted.

- Steroids (e.g., prednisone) may cause very high blood sugar levels and are often used for asthma. If prescribed, the diabetes care-provider should be notified.

- Suggestions for sick-day foods are given in Table 2.

- More importantly, in people with diabetes who have complications (eye, kidney, nerve, and heart disease), some medications should be avoided.

- Table 3 may help you decide when and whom to call for extra help.

Type 2 Diabetes

Youth with type 2 diabetes must also remember to check the urine and/or blood ketone level with any illness.

- If the person is receiving metformin (Glucophage), the pills should be stopped during the illness.

- It may be best to return to insulin shots during the illness.

- Call your doctor or nurse if you have questions.

SURGERY MANAGEMENT

If surgery is planned, call your diabetes care-provider AFTER you find out the time of the surgery and if eating food in usual amounts will be allowed.

Take your own diabetes supplies with you to the surgery, including:

- blood sugar meter and strips, with finger poker (lancet)

- CGM (if used) and extra sensor

- insulin and syringes

- glucose (dextrose) tablets or gel

- blood ketone strips and meter or urine Ketostix

- glucagon emergency kit

- if on a pump, equipment to change infusion set if needed

- your phone card with your diabetes care-provider's number

If you receive a basal insulin (e.g., by insulin pump or by Lantus, Levemir or Tresiba injection), the basal insulin can be continued during the period of surgery. Then restart bolus pump therapy or bolus insulin injections when the person is able to eat. Be sure to speak to the surgery team about blood sugar management.

TABLE 2

Sick-Day Foods

Liquids*

• Fruit juice: apple, cranberry, grape, grapefruit, orange, pineapple, etc.

• Sugar-containing beverages: regular 7Up®, ginger ale, orange juice, cola, PEPSI®, etc.*

• Fruit-flavored drinks: regular Kool-Aid, lemonade, Hi-C®, etc.*

• Sports drinks: Gatorade, POWERADE®, etc., any flavor

• Pedialyte, or Infalyte® (especially for younger children)

• JELL-O®: regular or diet

• Popsicles, regular or diet

• Broth-type soup: bouillon, chicken noodle soup, Cup-a-Soup®

Solids (when ready)

• Saltine crackers

• Banana (or other fruit)

• Applesauce

• Bread or toast

• Graham crackers

• Soup

***Sugar-free may be needed depending on blood/CGM glucose levels (e.g., greater than 150 mg/dL [8.3 mmol/L]).**

TABLE 3
Sick-Day Management:
When/Whom to Call for Emergency Care

• Call your family doctor if you have vomited three or more times and can keep nothing in your stomach, but urine ketones are not moderate or large or blood ketones above 1.0 mmol/L.

• If moderate or large ketones are present or blood ketones are above 1.0 mmol/L, call your diabetes care-provider if you have questions about treatment.

• *If help is needed with an insulin dose, call your diabetes care-provider.*

• If you have difficulty breathing or have rapid or deep breathing, you need to go to an emergency room immediately. This usually indicates severe acidosis (ketoacidosis; Chapter 15).

• Low blood sugar (hypoglycemia) can occur with vomiting or not eating normal amounts of food. More frequent blood sugar checks are important. If there is any unusual behavior such as confusion, slurred speech, double vision, inability to move or talk, or jerking, someone should give sugar or instant glucose. Check a blood sugar when possible. Glucagon (Chapter 6) is given if the person is unconscious or if a convulsion (seizure) occurs. The diabetes care-provider should be contacted if a severe reaction occurs. In case of a convulsion (seizure) or loss of consciousness, it may be necessary to call the paramedics or to go to an emergency room. Have an emergency number posted by the phone.

YOUR INSULIN DOSE MAY CHANGE WHEN YOU ARE SICK, BUT YOU ALWAYS NEED SOME INSULIN.

FAMILY SUPPORT IS VERY IMPORTANT FOR THE PERSON WITH DIABETES.

CHAPTER 17
FAMILY CONCERNS

Diabetes is a family disease. All family members need to work together to incorporate diabetes into their lives. This means that all family members must help. The people who do best with their diabetes have the help and support of all family members.

• It is important for children with diabetes to be treated just like other children. A rule to follow is:

THINK OF THE CHILD FIRST AND THE DIABETES SECOND.

• It is important that all family members share their feelings (see Chapter 10).

• Siblings often feel left out when the child with diabetes needs more attention. This should be discussed with the other children and time should be set aside for them as well.

• Perhaps the most supportive and loving act that parents, brothers and sisters can make for the person with diabetes is to remove high-sugar foods (candy, sugar pop, donuts, cookies, etc.) from the home. These foods have little nutritional value and are not healthy for any family members.

SPECIFIC AREAS OF CONCERN

• The stress of the diagnosis of diabetes is real for all family members. Any of the feelings discussed in Chapter 10 (e.g.: sadness, anger, guilt) may linger. They generally improve with time.

• One of the four big influences on blood sugar levels is stress (see Chapter 14). The psych-social team (social worker or psychologist) is available to help in dealing with stress and other feelings.

• Extra activity and excitement may cause low (or high) blood sugar levels in people with diabetes. Some of the following may include delayed meals as well as increased activity:

  • family picnics
  • sleepovers
  • trips to the beach or hiking
  • school field days or trips
  • a trip to Disney® or other theme parks
  • special days such as Christmas, Hanukkah or Ramadan

• Thinking ahead, adjusting the insulin dose, checking more blood/CGM glucose levels and giving extra snacks if sugar levels are low, may result in a better day for everyone.

• Wearing an ID bracelet (or other ID) is important.

• Needle fears occur in about one-fourth of all people. The psych-social team may be helpful, particularly in suggesting distractions (TV, toys, books) or relaxation techniques (also see Chapter 9). If family members have needle fears, the psych-social team may need to help.

- Missed shots (or insulin boluses for the pumper) result in an elevated HbA1c level and an increased risk for diabetic complications. Help from other family members, teachers, friends or counselors to remember injections may be needed.

- Driving a car with the threat of hypoglycemia can be a family concern relating to a person with diabetes, and is discussed in Chapter 20.

- Fear of hypoglycemia is common and must be dealt with or it may prevent optimal management of diabetes. Education may help alleviate this fear. The use of CGM (Chapter 29) is also often helpful. Recently, the FDA in the U.S. approved the first product combining a pump and CGM that stops insulin infusion when a person is hypoglycemic (see Chapter 30 for more details).

- Other behavioral issues (e.g., eating disorders) are discussed in the book, *"Understanding Diabetes."*

SOCIAL WORKERS AND PSYCHOLOGISTS ARE THERE TO HELP YOU.

THINK OF THE PERSON FIRST AND THEN THE DIABETES.

WHILE A LOW HbA1C AND MINIMAL LOW BLOOD SUGARS ARE TREATMENT GOALS, LEADING A FULL LIFE IS THE ULTIMATE GOAL.

HIGH OR LOW BLOOD SUGARS MAY AFFECT SCHOOL PERFORMANCE

CHAPTER 18
CARE OF CHILDREN AT DIFFERENT AGES

Children of different ages are able to handle different tasks and responsibilities. These may vary from day-to-day and week-to-week. This is true for diabetes-related tasks and non-diabetes tasks. Giving insulin injections for different aged children is discussed in Chapter 9. It can be helpful for family members to have an idea of what to expect at different ages. (See the Tables of age-responsibilities in the book, *"Understanding Diabetes,"* Chapter 18.) Goals for blood sugar levels and HbA1c values for children of different ages are included in Chapters 7 and 14.

BELOW AGE 8 YEARS

• Parents do all tasks.

• Children gradually learn to cooperate.

• Shots or boluses are often given after meals or snacks (rather than before) depending upon how reliably the child eats.

AGES 8-12 YEARS

• Children begin to give some of their own shots or assume pump-related activities/ responsibilities. A common mistake is to push for too much responsibility before the child is ready.

• Having a friend spend the night or staying at a friend's house often begins during this period. As the children are often very active and use more energy from staying up later than usual, it is best to reduce the insulin dose.

• At this age, fine motor control and the sense of accuracy needed to draw up the insulin develops.

• It is important to continue to check doses of insulin drawn by the child to make sure of accurate amounts. It is also important to check the blood/CGM glucose devices to review their readings.

• The idea of maintaining optimal sugar control to prevent later diabetes complications can initially be understood around ages 12 or 13 years.

AGES 13-18 YEARS

At this age, youth begin to have the ability to do all or most of their diabetes management. They may need reminders for checking blood sugars or taking insulin with food. One of the most difficult chores for many teens is writing the blood sugar values in a log book (or downloading meter or CGM results). It is important to do this or trends in blood/ CGM glucose values will be missed. Most glucose meters, pumps and CGMs can now be easily downloaded at home. Often the parents agree to do this (with the teen's OK). It is also a way for the parents to stay involved with the diabetes care and to step back in if blood/CGM glucose levels are not being evaluated. A decrease in the number of blood sugar checks per day is a major reason HbA1c levels tend to be higher in teenagers.

WHAT IS THE AGE WHEN SELF-CARE SHOULD HAPPEN?

- Children should be encouraged to assume self-care as they are able.

- There isn't a "magic" age when children should take over everything.

- If too much is expected too soon, feelings of failure and low self-esteem with poor diabetes self-care may result.

- **We believe that a supportive adult can be valuable for any person with diabetes, no matter the person's age.**

AN ALARM WATCH MAY HELP TO REMIND A CHILD OF THE NEED FOR A SNACK, OR TO GIVE A SHOT OF INSULIN.

CHILDREN BETWEEN THE AGES OF 8-14 CAN BEGIN TO HELP MANAGE THEIR DIABETES.

CHAPTER 19
DIABETES MANAGEMENT IN THE TODDLER/PRESCHOOLER

Chapter 18 deals with traits related and not-related to diabetes for different aged children including toddlers and preschoolers. Giving insulin shots to young children is discussed in Chapter 9. Although most of diabetes management is similar to that of older aged children, questions are often asked relating to insulin therapy.

BASAL-BOLUS INSULIN THERAPY (also see Chapter 8)

When possible, basal-bolus insulin therapy should be used in this age group. The use of NPH insulin is more apt to result in low blood/CGM glucose levels, particularly during the night.

The basal insulins are Lantus, Levemir (often given twice daily) and Tresiba (also called Degludec). They are often given once daily – preferably in the morning in toddlers. Then if the insulin does not last a full 24 hours, insulin activity is less in the early morning hours when lows are worrisome. Some parents give the injection (often in the buttocks) while the child is still asleep.

The preferred bolus insulin is either Humalog, NovoLog or Aprida. In contrast to older children, the shot is sometimes given after the meal if eating is unpredictable in this age group. The dose can then be chosen after seeing what the child eats. Blood/CGM glucose levels will then be higher after meals in comparison to giving the bolus 20 minutes before the meal. This is a compromise to avoid hypoglycemia. Smaller (3ml) vials of Humalog can be ordered from pharmacies.

The NDC number (to tell the pharmacist) is 002-7510-17. There is also a 3ml NovoLog FlexPen® and the NovoPen® Junior which gives 0.5 unit doses. Hopefully, the co-pay will also be less with lower amounts of insulin.

SUGAR CONTROL

The goals for blood/CGM glucose levels (80-200 mg/dL or 4.5-11.1 mmol/L) are not as strict for this age group in comparison to older children.

The goals for sugar control are less stringent in young children for several reasons:

• unpredictable eating

• inconsistent physical activity

• young children may not recognize or communicate hypoglycemic episodes

• the brain is still developing

• the risk for complication damage is low prior to puberty

Small doses of insulin can have big effects on blood sugar levels. The 2014 ADA goal for children of this age is to aim for an HbA1c level below 7.5 percent (<58 mmol/mol). This is considerably lower than in past years. The ISPAD (International Society for Pediatric and Adolescent Diabetes) goal is also to have the value <7.5 percent (<58 mmol/mol) for all ages of children. There is now some evidence that high blood sugars and episodes of ketoacidosis can also have adverse effects on the developing brain (as with low blood sugar). Both the ADA and ISPAD recommend HbA1c levels, "as appropriate for each child and family."

INSULIN PUMPS

About half of children in this age group in the U.S. are treated with insulin pumps. Advantages of insulin pumps (Chapter 28) are:

• frequent shots are avoided

• more precise dosing is possible

• ability to give multiple insulin doses with meals, snacks or high blood sugars

Several studies have shown that insulin pumps are safe in young children. The parents obviously do all of the pump management and must agree to wanting the pump for their child. For some parents, early pump use has been associated with more stress, although this usually lessens with time. The use of temporary basal rates or turning off the pump for periods of high activity or at the time of low blood/CGM glucose values can be advantageous. HbA1c levels may not always decrease with pump use in this age child. Other important reasons for pump use are safety and convenience.

CONTINUOUS GLUCOSE MONITORS (CGM)

As with pumps, a CGM can be used in this age group **when the family is ready** (see Chapter 29). This is particularly true for young children who cannot tell a parent when they are feeling high or low. The CGM provides convenience for the parents being able to see the glucose levels at any given time and in not having to do as many finger, toe or heel pokes for blood sugar levels. Some blood sugar checks will still be necessary. They are necessary for daily calibrations of the CGM, and should always be performed with high and low glucose level alarms. The

major drawback is adequate locations for the insertions, especially if also using an insulin pump. The diabetes nurse educator can help to explore this issue. A major advantage is that when used with the Medtronic 530G insulin pump, the Threshold (low glucose) Suspend feature can help to prevent severe hypoglycemia (see Chapter 30).

CHAPTER 20
SPECIAL CHALLENGES OF THE TEEN YEARS

The teen years are a time when young people go between wanting to be an independent adult and wanting to stay a dependent child. It is not surprising that they go back and forth when it comes to taking over the diabetes responsibilities. Many research studies now show that when parents stay involved in diabetes management, the diabetes will be in better control.

THE CHALLENGES

The teen-aged years are often the most difficult for having optimal sugar control (including a HbA1c value below 7.5 percent [58 mmol/mol]). And yet, they are important years in relation to an increased risk for diabetes complications.

If the number of blood sugar checks per day is reduced, the HbA1c level will rise.

Growth and sex hormones are at high levels and interfere with insulin activity.

Insulin pumps, more frequent insulin shots or boluses, or use of the basal insulins, Lantus, Levemir or Tresiba (Degludec) rather than NPH insulin can help some teens. However, if meal and snack shots (or boluses for pumpers) are missed, the HbA1c will increase.

Driving a car safely is very important beginning in the teen years. It is important to always check a blood/CGM glucose level before driving. Driving with a low blood sugar can result in problems that can be just as severe as if driving while drunk (see Chapter 20 in "*Understanding Diabetes*").

Diabetes is often not a priority to the teenager. Teenagers have special issues, including:

- **struggle for independence**

- **growth and body changes**

- **self-identity**

- **sports activities (see Chapter 13)**

- **peer relationships**

- **substance abuse (tobacco, alcohol, drugs, etc.)**

- **sexuality (including anticipatory guidance for birth control and safe sex)**

- **driving a car**

- **college**

- **emotional changes**

- **consistency**

Consistency is a key word in diabetes management. This may relate to food intake, exercise, stress, doing blood/CGM glucose levels and timing of insulin shots/boluses. It is often hard for teens to be consistent.

These are all discussed in detail in the book, "*Understanding Diabetes.*"

Parents must:

- **find ways to stay involved in diabetes management.** They can be helpful in keeping the log book, downloading meters, pumps or CGMs and in talking about insulin dosage.

- **be available to help, but should try not to be overbearing or constantly nagging.** A supportive adult can be helpful for a person with diabetes no matter the person's age.

- **help with communication to the diabetes care-providers.** This may involve sending meter, pump or CGM data by email or fax.

It is not surprising that diabetes is often referred to as a "disease of compromise."

TEENAGERS HAVE THEIR OWN SPECIAL CHALLENGES.

TEENAGERS WITH DIABETES CAN LEAD NORMAL LIVES.

NORMAL TEEN ACTIVITIES CAN PROVIDE MUCH-NEEDED EXERCISE.

CLINIC VISITS SHOULD BE EVERY THREE MONTHS FOR PEOPLE WITH DIABETES.

CHAPTER 21
OUTPATIENT MANAGEMENT, SUPPORT GROUPS, EDUCATION, AND STANDARDS OF CARE

WHAT SHOULD HAPPEN AFTER A DIAGNOSIS OF DIABETES?

After initial education, people with diabetes should receive regular follow-up visits every three months. Diabetes education should continue for the patient and family at these visits.

The insulin doses may be changed during these visits. As children grow they need more insulin. It is usually increased one-half unit per pound of weight gained.

On the physical exam, thyroid size and eye changes are checked. Growth and other signs of sugar control are also checked. If blood/CGM glucose values have been high, the sugar may collect on the joint proteins and finger curvatures may result.

The HbA1c level (see Chapter 14) should be done every three months.

According to the ADA, screening for the eyes (eye exam) and kidneys (urine microalbumins) should be done annually for people who have had type 1 diabetes for five or more years, starting at age 10 years or at puberty, whichever is first.

For people with type 2 diabetes, the eye and kidney evaluations should be done at the time of diagnosis, and then yearly.

WHAT ELSE IS IMPORTANT?

Communication (fax, email) of blood/CGM glucose values to the healthcare provider is often helpful (to receive suggestions for insulin dose changes).

Clinic visits by telemedicine are now available in some areas. These should be alternated with regular clinic visits so physical exam changes can be checked.

The families should let their diabetes provider or diabetes team know about any of the following:

• any severe low blood sugar (hypoglycemic) reactions (with loss of consciousness or seizure)

• frequent mild reactions

• moderate or large urine ketones or blood ketones above 1.0 mmol/L

• any planned surgery

• if at least half of the blood/CGM glucose values are not in the desired range for age (see Chapter 7)

SUPPORT GROUPS AND CONTINUING EDUCATION

Support groups, age-related group clinics, and special educational programs (Research Updates, Carb Counting Class, Pump or CGM classes, Grandparents Workshop, College-Bound Workshop, etc.) are available in many areas.

Special events (family workshops, bike trips, camps, a Halloween party, etc.) help children and families to learn more about diabetes.

They also provide a chance to talk to others who have a family member with diabetes.

There are many excellent websites for people and families with diabetes. Some that we recommend are:

- www.childrenwithdiabetes.com
- www.childrensdiabetesfoundation.org
- www.barbaradaviscenter.org
- www.jdrf.org
- www.diabetes.org
- www.myglu.org

STANDARDS OF CARE

The ADA "Standards of Care" are published each January as a supplement to the journal, Diabetes Care. The ISPAD guidelines are published in Pediatric Diabetes. The diabetes care team should be up-to-date on these standards. They can be found online.

FAXING OR EMAILING BLOOD/CGM GLUCOSE VALUES TO THE CLINIC BETWEEN VISITS IS VERY IMPORTANT.

MARK YOUR CALENDAR TO REMIND YOU OF FOLLOW-UP VISITS EVERY THREE MONTHS.

ASK IF YOU NEED HELP CHANGING YOUR DOSE!

CHAPTER 22
ADJUSTING INSULIN DOSAGES

We encourage patients and families to learn to change the insulin doses on their own. Your diabetes care team is available if you have questions.

HOW AND WHEN SHOULD AN INSULIN DOSE BE CHANGED?

1. Looking at blood/CGM glucose patterns over the last week allows changes to be made.

It is necessary to know which insulin is acting at the time of the highs or lows in order to make the correct changes (see Figures in Chapter 8).

If more than half of the blood/CGM glucose values at any time of the day are above the desired range for the age of the person (see Table in Chapter 7), the insulin dose acting at the time of the high blood sugar values should be increased. If values are still high after three days, the dose can be increased again.

If changing basal rates on an insulin pump, remember that the insulin peaks in 90 minutes, so the dose must be increased or decreased an hour before the time of concern.

If there are more than two lows (below 60 mg/dL [3.3 mmol/L]) at one time of day, the insulin dose acting at that time should be decreased. If more lows occur, the dose can be decreased again the next day.

2. The change in insulin dose will vary by age and "insulin sensitivity."

With small children, the change in dose may be by one half to one unit.

With older children and teens, the change in dose may be by one or two units.

Tables are given in the larger book, *"Understanding Diabetes"* (Chapter 22) for people wanting more detailed suggestions on changing insulin doses for high or low blood sugar values.

3. Correction (or sensitivity) factors are used to help adjust each insulin dose.

The correction (or sensitivity) factor refers to the number of units of insulin needed to correct or reduce a blood sugar to a desired level.

The **correction factor** can be used to "correct" a high blood sugar down to a **target blood/CGM glucose level** (e.g., 150 mg/dL [8.3 mmol/L] during the night and 120 mg/dL [6.7 mmol/L] during the day).

One example of a **correction factor** is to give one unit of insulin for every 50 mg/dL (2.8 mmol/L) of glucose above 150 mg/dL (8.3 mmol/L); e.g., if the blood/CGM glucose level is 250 mg/dL (13.9 mmol/L), the correction factor is 2 units. Many teens and adults correct down to 120 mg/dL (6.7 mmol/L) or even 100 mg/dL (5.5 mmol/L) during the day. However, every person is different and the correction factor should be adjusted to fit the individual.

If the correction factor being used is the correct dose, blood sugar levels should be at target (corrected) after two to three hours. If this does not happen, the correction factor may need to be changed (e.g., from 1 unit per 50 mg/dL [2.8 mmol/L] to 1 unit per 30 mg/dL [1.7 mmol/L]).

At bedtime, during the night, or before exercise, the correction factor is often reduced by half.

It is generally wise to wait two hours between correction insulin dosages to allow the rapid-acting insulin to have its effect.

Most people use a combination of a **correction factor** and an **insulin to carbohydrate (carb) ratio** (see Chapter 12) dose to determine the total dose of rapid-acting insulin before meals and snacks (see Table).

4. Changes in Insulin dosages for food are discussed in Chapter 12.

Meal boluses are usually chosen based on the carbs to be eaten. The insulin to carbohydrate (I/C) ratios for different meals may be chosen by the dietitian or other diabetes team members.

One of the greatest deficiencies in diabetes management relates to a lack of blood sugar checks two and four hours after meals. The ADA recommends that all values be below 180 mg/dL (10 mmol/L). The use of a continuous glucose monitor (CGM) can be a great aid in evaluating post-meal sugar levels.

The methods to increase or decrease I/C ratios are given in Chapter 12.

With the current rapid-acting insulins, giving the dose 20 minutes before eating is often very effective in lowering post-meal sugar levels (Chapter 8).

5. Changes for Lantus, Levemir or Tresiba (Degludec) are based on similar factors.

Adjustments are usually made based on the morning (fasting) blood sugar levels.

Doses are increased or decreased if blood sugar levels are consistently above or below the recommended fasting values for age (see Chapter 7).

As suggested above, dose changes for a young child may be by one half to one unit, and for older children (and teens) by one to two units.

Suggested waiting times between dose changes are 3-4 days unless follow-up blood sugar values are <70 or >300 mg/dL (<3.9 or >16.7 mmol/L). If this is the case, more frequent corrections can be made.

6. The use of "thinking" scales will allow further insulin adjustment.

The insulin dose is figured by considering many factors, including:

• the blood/CGM glucose level

• if using CGM, the arrow and the direction of glucose change

• illness

• any exercise that has been or is to be done

• stress

• food to be eaten

• menses

Families gradually learn to make insulin adjustments based on these factors.

It is VERY important to make insulin adjustments between visits if blood sugars are not in range half of the time or if low more than 10 percent of the time. Your diabetes care team is available if you have questions.

TABLE

Example of Determining an Insulin Dose

Blood Sugar		Correction Factor**	Carbohydrates***		Total Units
mg/dL	mmol/L	Units of Insulin	Grams	Units of Insulin	of Insulin
<150*	<8.3*	0	(15g)	1	1
200	11.1	1	(30g)	2	3
250	13.9	2	(45g)	3	5
300	16.7	3	(60g)	4	7
350	19.4	4	(75g)	5	9

* < = means "less than"

**Assuming a correction factor of 1 unit of rapid-acting insulin per 50 mg/dL (2.8 mmol/L) above 150 mg/dL (8.3 mmol/L).

*** In this example, 1 unit of insulin is given for each 15g of carbs. The carbs are increased by 15g for each line in the Table.

THE INSULIN DOSE MAY NEED TO CHANGE WITH THE AMOUNT OF FOOD EATEN OR WITH SPORTS ACTIVITIES ("THINKING" SCALE).

CHAPTER 23
LONG-TERM COMPLICATIONS OF DIABETES

WHAT CAN REDUCE THE RISK OF DIABETES COMPLICATIONS?

- Optimal blood sugar control will reduce the risk for eye, kidney, nerve, and heart complications of diabetes by more than 50 percent, as shown by the DCCT (Chapter 14).

- Not smoking (or chewing) tobacco also helps.

- Other factors include elevated blood pressure or blood lipids (e.g., cholesterol). Even mild increases in blood pressure can damage the eyes and kidneys.

- Maintaining a healthy diet and weight (with exercise) is important.

- Optimal diabetes management reduces the risk of future complications.

HOW ARE COMPLICATIONS FOUND?

Small Blood Vessels (Eyes, Kidneys and Nerves)

- Regular eye exams (and especially photographs) by the eye doctor tell if someone is developing eye damage.

- The urine microalbumin determination tells if someone is getting early kidney damage at a time when it may still be reversible.

- According to the ADA, screening for the eyes (eye exam) and kidneys (urine microalbumins) should be done annually for people who have had type 1 diabetes for five or more years starting at age 10 years or at puberty, whichever is first.

- People who have type 2 diabetes should have the eye and kidney evaluations done soon after diagnosis and then every year.

- Families may need to help remind the healthcare team that it is time to do the annual microalbumin screen or to see an eye doctor.

- Neuropathy screening is done as a part of the physical exam.

Large Blood Vessels (Including the Heart [Coronary] Blood Vessels)

- Heart attacks and other blood vessel diseases are a greater risk in adults with diabetes. Long term optimal sugar control is important in prevention.

- Avoiding tobacco use is important for **ALL** people, but especially for people with diabetes.

- Maintenance of normal weight, blood pressure and cholesterol is also important in prevention.

- Cholesterol (lipid) levels should be screened at puberty, or sooner if there is a family history of high cholesterol.

- Adult diabetes clinics usually do special evaluations of the heart (EKG's) and blood vessels at regular intervals.

- Risk factors and aims for prevention are summarized in the Table.

TREATMENT

- The most important treatment of early complications involves improving sugar control. Maintaining normal weight, blood pressure, and cholesterol levels is also important.

- Treatment of early kidney damage is often helped by lowering elevations in blood pressure. A blood pressure medicine called an ACE-inhibitor is often used initially.

- If many eye changes are present, laser treatment to the back of the eye (retina) may help prevent more severe problems.

TABLE
Heart and Blood Vessel Risk Factors

Risk Factors	Aim for Prevention
glucose (sugar) control	HbA1c in recommended range for age
blood pressure	below 140/80 or 90th percentile for age
tobacco use	don't use
elevated total cholesterol	below 200 mg/dL (5.2 mmol/L)
elevated LDL cholesterol	below 100 mg/dL (2.6 mmol/L)
elevated (fasting) triglyceride	below 150 mg/dL (1.7 mmol/L)

If any of the levels are elevated, it is important to discuss with your physician.

DO NOT SMOKE!
(OR CHEW TOBACCO!)

CHAPTER 24
ASSOCIATED AUTOIMMUNE CONDITIONS OF TYPE 1 DIABETES

Other autoimmune (self-allergy) diseases are also associated with type 1 diabetes. This is due to the inheritance of genes increasing the risk for autoimmunity (associated with both type 1 diabetes and these diseases). Three examples of autoimmune diseases seen more frequently in people with type 1 diabetes are discussed below.

THYROID PROBLEMS

Thyroid problems (like type 1 diabetes) are partly due to autoimmunity (see Chapter 3). Antibodies are made against the thyroid gland. About 1 in 20 people with diabetes need treatment with a daily thyroid hormone replacement pill.

We recommend careful examination of the thyroid gland with clinic visits every three months. Laboratory evaluations should be done annually, particularly if the thyroid gland is enlarged or if there is any fall-off in height attainment. The TSH (**T**hyroid **S**timulating **H**ormone) is the best laboratory value for screening. Some physicians also order a blood thyroid hormone level (T4 or free T4).

CELIAC DISEASE

This involves an allergy to the protein gluten, present in wheat, barley and rye. It occurs in approximately 1 of every 20 people with diabetes. There may be stomach complaints (pain, gas, diarrhea) or poor growth. Half of the people with celiac disease have no symptoms.

We recommend routine screening of all people with type 1 diabetes with the blood transglutaminase level (or other assays). If positive, it is important to work closely with GI (gastrointestinal) physicians. If the person with diabetes is positive, other family members should also be screened. The treatment is to remove all wheat, rye and barley products from the diet. Meeting with a dietitian is important. Websites for obtaining more information on celiac disease and foods to avoid are given in Chapter 24 of "*Understanding Diabetes.*"

ADRENAL DISORDERS

Autoimmunity against the adrenal gland (Addison's disease) can occur, but is quite rare (1 in 500 people with type 1 diabetes). Low adrenal gland function can be treated with hormone replacement pills and is important to diagnose if present. Cortisol, the hormone the body is unable to produce in Addison's disease, is especially important during body stress (e.g., surgery or a serious infection). Addison's disease can be life-threatening if untreated.

MAKE SURE THAT YOU HAVE SNACKS
HANDY AT SCHOOL IN CASE YOU NEED THEM.

CHAPTER 25
THE SCHOOL OR WORK AND DIABETES

WHAT SHOULD BE DONE?

Most schools now require school health plans. Schools in Colorado use a basic "Standard of Care" for diabetes management for all youth (Table 1). The diabetes team fills out the "Healthcare Provider Order for Student with Diabetes," depending on whether using insulin injections (Table 2) or an insulin pump (Table 3). An Individualized School Health Plan or **IHP** is then filled out by the parents and the school nurse or aide. An example of the IHP is available in *"Understanding Diabetes"* if the school nurse does not have one. You are welcome to copy the Tables in this chapter.

The parents must also provide supplies for the school (see Table 4). Some children keep a separate meter and strips at the school. Others bring their home-meter and supplies in their backpack.

Other forms that you may want to copy from *"Understanding Diabetes"* (Chapter 25) are:

1) Individualized Health Plan (IHP)

2) Individualized Health Plan – School Nurse Checklist

3) Insulin Pumps in the School Setting

4) Continuous Glucose Monitoring (CGM) in the School

WHAT CAN HAPPEN AT SCHOOL?

- Low blood sugars are the most likely emergency to occur at school. Treatment is reviewed in Table 1. If a child leaves the classroom while having a low blood sugar, they **must** have someone with them. It may be helpful for the family to copy and review the Table on mild, moderate and severe reactions with the school (see Chapter 6). *Supplies for treating lows will also need to be provided by the family.*

- High blood sugars and/or ketones may also occur at school, particularly with stress, illness, menses, overeating or lack of exercise. If the blood/CGM glucose level is above 300 mg/dL (16.7 mmol/L) on two checks (≈ 1 hour apart), the urine or blood ketones need to be checked. When the blood sugar is high it is generally necessary to go to the bathroom more frequently. Treatment for high blood sugar is reviewed in Table 1. *If urine ketones are positive or blood ketones are above 0.6 mmol/L, the parents need to be called.*

WORK

People with diabetes must have all necessary diabetes supplies and snacks readily available at work. The American Disabilities Act states that employers must provide, "reasonable accommodations to allow a person with diabetes to safely and successfully perform their job." Friends, family and some co-workers and/or supervisors need to know about the diabetes and, at a minimum, what to do in case help is needed for a low blood sugar. An emergency plan to provide essential details is included at the end of Chapter 14 in the book *"Management of Diabetes in Adults"* (see ordering material available in the back of this book).

TABLE 1
Standards of Care for Diabetes Management in the School Setting

These are general standards of care for students with Type 1 Diabetes to be used in conjunction with the Provider Orders and Individualized Health Plans. The student's healthcare-provider may indicate exceptions to these standards on the student's individual orders.

1. Communication: To facilitate appropriate execution of the healthcare-provider's orders and to ensure safety of the student, the School Nurse will have authorization to exchange health information with the provider to assist in developing, updating and carrying out the Individualized Health Plan.

2. Monitoring Blood Glucose (BG): *The student's healthcare-provider should indicate individualized blood glucose target ranges on the student's individual orders.*

Standard Target Ranges Before Meals: (unless otherwise indicated on Provider orders)

< 5 y.o.	80-200 mg/dl (4.4-11.1 mmol/L)
5-11 y.o.	70-180 mg/dl (3.9-10.0 mmol/L)
12-18 y.o.	70-150 mg/dl (3.9-8.3 mmol/L)
>18 y.o.	70-130 mg/dl (3.9-7.2 mmol/L)

Notification to Parents:

Low < _____ and **High > 300** mg/dl (16.7 mmol/L)(or individualized based on orders)

Note: The frequency of routine BG monitoring should take into consideration the student's schedule and participation in classroom learning/activities. Too frequent routine glucose monitoring may impact learning and school participation. On average, a student would have routine glucose monitoring one to three times/day at school

3. Hypoglycemia (Low Blood Sugar)
Treatment for Hypoglycemia

- Student should be treated in the classroom if symptomatic or if BG is below *Target Range*. If the student needs to go to the Health Office – he/she should be accompanied.

- Check BG - if meter not available, treat symptoms.

- If BG is below *Target Range* and/or student is symptomatic, treat with ~15 gram fast-acting carbohydrate (e.g. 4 dextrose tablets). **Re-test** in 10-15 minutes. Repeat 15gm fast-acting carbohydrate until BG is within *Target Range*. Follow with snack or lunch.

- At lunchtime, after BG is within *Target Range,* send the student to lunch and give insulin after eating, unless otherwise indicated on healthcare-provider orders.

- **Mild symptoms:** Check BG, treat with juice, glucose tabs, etc. until BG is within *Target Range*. Follow with snack/lunch.

- **Moderate symptoms:** if unable to drink juice, administer glucose gel. Re-test every 15 minutes until BG is within *Target Range*. Follow with snack or lunch (see Note below).

- **Severe symptoms** which may include seizures, unconscious, unable or unwilling to take juice or gel:

- **Administer Glucagon** if trained staff is available and **call 911.** Disconnect/suspend pump. *< 16 years old = 0.5 cc and ≥ 16 years = 1.0 cc* IM *(unless otherwise indicated by provider)*

Note: Do not give insulin for carbohydrates taken to <u>treat</u> low BG. For the student who is on a pump, the School Nurse should discuss with the parent whether the student is given an insulin bolus for snacks following hypoglycemia and note on Individualized Health Plan.

4. Hyperglycemia (High Blood Sugar)
Treatment for Hyperglycemia

- Check urine/blood ketones if BG is over 300 mg/dl twice in a row (≈ 1 hour apart) or with symptoms of illness/vomiting. If any ketones are present, provide water and call parents. If > 2.5 hours since last dose of

Table 1 (continued)

insulin, the student may need insulin via injection (School Nurse should call healthcare-provider for one-time orders if the student only has orders for correction at lunchtime).

- Students can stay in the school and participate in classroom activities with hyperglycemia if they are not symptomatic and/or do not have moderate/large ketones.
- If ketones are present, call parents, provide water, prohibit exercise (see Exercise below).
- Recommend the student be released from school when urine ketones are moderate/large or with symptoms of illness in order to be treated and monitored more closely by parent/guardian.

With Pump:

- The student *may* require insulin via injection and a new infusion site/set (to be changed by parent/guardian or independent student). School Nurse should call parent and healthcare-provider if this occurs to determine insulin and/or set change required. The concern is a malfunctioning infusion set with the risk of going into Diabetic Ketoacidosis (DKA).
- Contact school nurse and parent for further instructions regarding insulin by injection or new infusion set.

Exercise:

- If the student has BGs in range or high and has only trace or small ketones, it is okay to exercise. If the ketones are moderate or large the student should not exercise. Note: always check BG and ketones before exercise if the student is not feeling well.

5. Continuous Glucose Monitors (CGM)

- CGM systems use a tiny sensor inserted under the skin to check glucose (sugar) levels in interstitial fluid. They may be used on an ongoing basis or for a short time to identify specific patient glucose levels and trends. The CGM is calibrated to the student using a finger stick glucose.
- Since the FDA has not approved CGM for treatment in pediatrics, glucose levels must be confirmed with a finger stick/meter before making a change in treatment. *Under NO circumstances should the CGM reading be used to give an insulin dose or treat a low/high BG. Always check finger stick BG level regardless of CGM reading.*
- Sensors remain in place from ≈ 3 days to a week. Parents are responsible for changing sensor/site.
- Parents will set the alarms and notify the school nurse of the parameters. Alarms should be used conservatively so as not to unnecessarily disrupt the student's school activities. They could be set on vibrate.
- Trend arrows showing lows/pending lows or highs/pending highs should be confirmed with a blood glucose meter and treated per healthcare plan/provider orders.

6. Insulin Management

- Fast acting insulins are interchangeable (e.g., Humalog, Novolog, Apidra) unless student is allergic to a certain brand or otherwise indicated.
- The parent and/or healthcare-provider should contact the school nurse for changes in insulin dosing.

7. Pump Management

- The computerized features/calculator set in the pump should be used for insulin boluses.
- All pump safety features should be operational in the school setting.

8. Self-Care Management

- Ability level to be determined by school nurse and parent unless Provider indicates otherwise on orders.
- All students, regardless of age or expertise, require a plan and may need assistance with hypoglycemia and illness.

(≈ = Approximately)

I agree with this standard of care.

Signed: _____   Date: _____
                                 Parent

Students with Diabetes in Colorado Schools Collaborative

TABLE 2

Healthcare-Provider Order for Student with Diabetes Using Injections

Student: _____ DOB: _____ School: _____ Grade: _____

Physician: _____ Phone: _____

Diabetes Educator: _____

Parent name(s) and phone number(s) _____

_____

Monitor Blood Glucose (Sugar):

Monitor (check all that apply):

☐ Before Lunch   ☐ Before Snack

☐ After Lunch   ☐ Before leaving to get on bus/going home

☐ Before PE   ☐ As needed for signs/symptoms of high BG

☐ After PE   ☐ Other:_____

Blood glucose (**BG**) at which parent should be notified: Low <_____ and High >_____.

Student **target range for BG** is _____.

The following two sections can be skipped if the school has adopted the Standards of Care (Table 1)

Hypoglycemia: Use Standards of Care for Diabetes Management in the School Setting, or Other (see below):

✓ If symptomatic but glucose meter not available, treat as indicated for symptoms below.

✓ If blood glucose in range _____ – _____ but symptomatic, treat with 10 to 15 gm carbohydrate snack.

✓ If mild symptoms (e.g., shaky, hungry, pale) test BG and if <_____, treat with juice, glucose tabs, etc. every 10-15 min. until BG above _____. Then give 10-15 gm carb snack or lunch.

✓ If moderate symptoms (e.g., not thinking clearly), they may be unable to drink independently. Test BG and administer sugar drink or glucose gel. Re-test and give a source of sugar every 15 minutes until BG above _____. Then give 10-15 gm carb snack or give lunch.

If severe reaction (seizure, unconscious), test BG and administer Glucagon _____unit(s) (___cc/ml) IM into thigh. *Give nothing by mouth! **CALL 911 AND PARENT.***

Do not give insulin for carbs to treat hypoglycemia until BG is > _____ and student has eaten.

Hyperglycemia and Ketone Testing: Use Standards of Care for Diabetes Management in the School Setting, or Other (see below):

☐ If BG >300 mg/dl (16.7 mmol/L) on two checks ≈ 1 hour apart, or illness/vomiting, TEST KETONES. If ketones present, student may require insulin injection.

☐ First, contact parent. Then call healthcare-provider for further instructions. Check ☐ blood ☐ urine ketones.

☐ If ketones present, call parent, provide water and keep student from exercise.

☐ Recommend student be released from school when ketones are moderate/large or has symptoms of illness, in order to be treated and monitored more closely by parent/guardian.

(≈ = Approximately)

Table 2 (continued)

Student's Self Care: (Ability level determined by school nurse and parent with input by healthcare-provider)

Needs assistance with pump management	☐ Yes	☐ No
Independently administers insulin	☐ Yes	☐ No
Independently monitors blood glucose	☐ Yes	☐ No
Independently treats mild hypoglycemia	☐ Yes	☐ No
Independently counts carbohydrates	☐ Yes	☐ No
Tests and interprets urine/blood ketones	☐ Yes	☐ No
Independently manages insulin boluses	☐ Yes	☐ No
Self injects with verification of dosage	☐ Yes	☐ No
Independently inserts infusion sets	☐ Yes	☐ No
Injections to be done by trained staff	☐ Yes	☐ No
Troubleshoots all alarms	☐ Yes	☐ No

Insulin Dose:
(Insulin to Carbohydrate ratio dose plus the sensitivity/correction factor dose):

Insulin to Carbohydrate ratio
_____unit of insulin per _____ grams of carbohydrate. Bolus for carbohydrates should occur ≈ 20 minutes before lunch, immediately before lunch, after lunch, ½ bolus before and ½ bolus after (circle one).

Sensitivity/Correction Factor Dose:
Upper target blood glucose: _____
_____ unit of insulin for every _____ mg/dl (mmol/L) above the Target Blood Glucose Range.

Comments:

Parent Authorization:

☐ Parent/Guardian authorized to increase/decrease sliding scale within _____units of insulin.

☐ Parent/Guardian authorized to increase/decrease insulin-to-carb ratio within: _____ unit/prescribed grams of carbs +/- _____ grams of carbs.

Adjustments not to exceed more than three times in one week for BGs below the target range, and not to exceed more than two times in one week for BGs above the target range.

SIGNATURES

My signature below provides authorization for the above written orders and exchange of health information to assist the school nurse in developing an Individual Health Plan. I understand that all procedures will be implemented in accordance with state laws and regulations and may be performed by unlicensed school personnel under the training and supervision provided by the school nurse. This order is for a maximum of one year.

Physician: _____ Date: _____

Parent: _____ Date: _____

School Nurse: _____ Date: _____

TABLE 3

Healthcare-Provider Order for Student with Diabetes Using a Pump

Student: _____ DOB: _____ School: _____ Grade: _____

Physician: _____ Phone: _____

Diabetes Educator: _____

Parent name(s) and phone number(s) _____

_____

Monitor Blood Glucose (Sugar):

Monitor (check all that apply):

☐ Before Lunch   ☐ Before Snack

☐ After Lunch   ☐ Before leaving to get on bus/going home

☐ Before PE   ☐ As needed for signs/symptoms of high BG

☐ After PE   ☐ Other:_____

Blood glucose (**BG**) at which parent should be notified: Low <_____ and High >_____.

Student **target range for BG** is _____.

The following two sections can be skipped if the school has adopted the Standards of Care (Table 1)

Hypoglycemia: Use Standards of Care for Diabetes Management in the School Setting, or Other (see below):

✓ Student should be accompanied to health office if symptomatic or BG <_____.

✓ If symptomatic but glucose meter not available, treat as indicated for symptoms below.

✓ If blood glucose in range _____ – _____ but symptomatic, treat with 10 to 15 gm carbohydrate snack.

✓ If mild symptoms (e.g., shaky, hungry, pale) test BG and if <_____, treat with juice, glucose tabs, etc. every 10-15 min. until BG above _____. Then give 10-15 gm carb snack or lunch.

✓ If moderate symptoms (e.g., not thinking clearly), they may be unable to drink independently. Test BG and administer sugar drink or glucose gel. Re-test and give a source of sugar every 15 minutes until BG above _____. Then give 10-15 gm carb snack or lunch.

If severe reaction (seizure, unconscious), test BG and administer Glucagon _____unit(s) (___cc/ml) IM into thigh. *Give nothing by mouth!* **SUSPEND OR DISCONNECT PUMP. CALL 911 AND PARENT.**

Do not bolus for carbohydrates given to treat hypoglycemia until BG is > _____ mg/dl, and student has eaten.

Hyperglycemia and Ketone Testing: Use Standards of Care for Diabetes Management in the School Setting, or Other (see below):

☐ If BG >300 mg/dl (16.7 mmol/L) on two checks ≈ 1 hour apart, or illness/vomiting, TEST KETONES. If ketones present, student may require insulin injection.

☐ First, contact parent. Then call healthcare-provider for further instructions. Check ☐ blood ☐ urine ketones.

☐ If ketones present, call parent, provide water and keep student from exercise.

☐ Recommend student be released from school when ketones are moderate/large or has symptoms of illness, in order to be treated and monitored more closely by parent/guardian.

(≈ = Approximately)

Table 3 (continued)

Student's Self Care: (Ability level determined by school nurse and parent with input by healthcare-provider)

Needs assistance with pump management	☐ Yes	☐ No
Independently administers insulin	☐ Yes	☐ No
Independently monitors blood glucose	☐ Yes	☐ No
Independently treats mild hypoglycemia	☐ Yes	☐ No
Independently counts carbohydrates	☐ Yes	☐ No
Tests and interprets urine/blood ketones	☐ Yes	☐ No
Independently manages pump boluses	☐ Yes	☐ No
Self injects with verification of dosage	☐ Yes	☐ No
Independently inserts infusion sets	☐ Yes	☐ No
Injections to be done by trained staff	☐ Yes	☐ No
Troubleshoots all alarms	☐ Yes	☐ No

Pump Insulin Dosing Orders (Insulin-to-Carb Ratios Plus the High BG Correction)

Insulin to Carbohydrate ratio dose:
_____unit of insulin per _____ grams of carbohydrate. Bolus for carbohydrates should occur ≈ 20 minutes before lunch, immediately before lunch, after lunch, ½ bolus before and ½ bolus after (circle one).

Sensitivity/Correction Factor Dose:
_____ unit of insulin for every _____ mg/dl (mmol/L) above the upper Target Blood Glucose Range.

Pump Malfunctions:
Disconnect pump when malfunctioning.

Insulin Dose:
If pump is operational, calculate insulin dose by using the pump bolus calculator, then give insulin dose via injection.
If pump is not operational:
☐ Give insulin as indicated here: _____
☐ Call parent and healthcare-provider (for orders)
☐ Give insulin according to Insulin to Carbohydrate Ratio and Correction Factor (see above).

Comments:

Parent/Guardian authorized to increase/decrease insulin-to-carb ratio within: 1 unit/prescribed grams of carbs +/- 5 grams of carbs. Adjustments not to exceed more than three times in one week for BGs below the target range, and not to exceed more than two times in one week for BGs above the target range.

SIGNATURES

My signature below provides authorization for the above written orders and exchange of health information to assist the school nurse in developing an Individual Health Plan. I understand that all procedures will be implemented in accordance with state laws and regulations and may be performed by unlicensed school personnel under the training and supervision provided by the school nurse. This order is for a maximum of one year.

Physician: _____ Date: _____

Parent: _____ Date: _____

School Nurse: _____ Date: _____

TABLE 4

School Diabetes Management and Supply Checklist for Parents

_____ Discuss specific care of your child with the teachers, school nurse, bus driver, coaches and other staff who will be involved.

_____ Complete the individualized school health care plan with the help of the school staff (using the healthcare-provider order form from the diabetes team).

_____ Make sure your child understands the details of who will help him/her with blood sugars, shots and treatment of high or low sugars at school and where supplies will be kept. Supplies should be kept in a place where they are always available if needed.

_____ Make arrangements for the school to send home blood sugar records weekly.

_____ Keep current phone numbers where you can be reached. Collect equipment for school: meter, strips and finger-poker, lancets, insulin, insulin syringes or pen, biohazard container, log book or a copy of blood sugar record form, extra insulin pump supplies, urine or blood ketone strips, photo for substitute teacher's folder.

_____ Food and drinks; parents need to check intermittently to make sure the following supplies are available:

- juice cans or boxes (approximately 15g of carb each)

- glucose tablets (and instructions to give 4 tablets for low blood sugar)

- instant glucose or cake decorating gel

- crackers (± peanut butter and/or cheese)

- quarters to buy sugar pop (soda) if needed

- Fruit Roll-Ups

- dried fruit

- raisins or other snacks

_____ Box with the child's name to store these food and drink items

Parents want to know that their child is in safe hands while at school. It is the parents' responsibility (not the child's) to inform and educate the school. Parents also want to make sure their child is not treated differently as a result of having diabetes.

CHAPTER 26
CHILD-SITTERS, GRANDPARENTS AND DIABETES

I t is important for parents to feel that their child is safe with caregivers other than the parents. It is also important for these caregivers to feel confident that they can provide diabetes care.

WHAT DO THEY NEED TO KNOW?

How much training is needed will depend upon the amount of time the child will be with the caregiver and the age of the child.

All caregivers need:

• some information about signs of low blood sugar and how to treat. Being prepared for a low blood sugar is essential.

• some basic instruction on foods and diabetes. A handout is in this chapter which can be cut out or copied for the caregiver.

• emergency phone numbers in case the parents cannot be reached. This helps everyone feel better.

• to know how to give shots, when to check for urine or blood ketones, and other more detailed information if the parents are to be away for a longer time period. It may be easier to learn to give the insulin(s) using an insulin pen.

• an extra supply of insulin, etc. (in case a bottle is dropped and broken). An extra glucagon kit (and knowing where it is kept) is also helpful.

Attending a "Grandparent Workshop" or other workshop can help to teach the grandparents, baby-sitters or other caregivers about diabetes.

• It is important for the child and the grandparents to continue to have a close relationship.

• It can also help to remove any fears about giving shots or treating low blood sugars.

Caregivers may wish to join the parents at initial education classes or at the time of clinic visits. They are always welcome.

INFORMATION FOR THE SITTER OR GRANDPARENT

Our child, _____, has diabetes.

Children with diabetes are generally normal and healthy. In a child who has diabetes, sugar cannot be used by the body because the pancreas no longer makes the hormone insulin. Because of this, daily insulin injections or an insulin pump are needed. Diabetes is not contagious. Caring for a child with diabetes does require a small amount of extra knowledge.

LOW BLOOD SUGAR

The only emergency that could come on quickly is LOW BLOOD SUGAR (otherwise known as "hypoglycemia" or an "insulin reaction"). This can occur if the child gets more exercise than usual or does not eat as much as usual. *The warning signs of low blood sugar vary (see Chapter 6) but may include any of the following*:

1. Hunger
2. Paleness, sweating, shaking
3. Eyes appear glassy, dilated or "big" pupils
4. Pale or flushed face
5. Personality changes such as crying or stubbornness
6. Headaches
7. Inattention, drowsiness, sleepiness at an unusual time
8. Weakness, irritability, confusion
9. Speech and coordination changes
10. If not treated, loss of consciousness and/or seizure

The signs our child usually has are: _____

_____

_____

Blood Sugar: It is ideal to check the blood sugar if this is possible. It takes 10-15 minutes for the blood sugar to increase after taking liquids with sugar. Thus, the blood sugar can even be done after taking sugar. If it is not convenient to check the blood sugar, go ahead with treatment anyway.

Treatment: Give SUGAR (preferably in a liquid form) to help the blood sugar rise.

You may give any of the following:
1. One-half cup of soft drink that contains sugar – **NOT a diet pop**
2. Three or four glucose tablets, sugar packets or cubes
3. One-half cup of fruit juice
4. LIFE-SAVERS (FIVE or SIX pieces) or other candy that has a low choking risk
5. One-half tube of Insta-Glucose or cake decorating gel (see below)

We usually treat reactions with: _____

_____

(copy as needed)

If the child is having a low blood sugar and he/she refuses to eat or has difficulty eating, give Insta-Glucose, cake decorating gel (1/2 tube) or other sugar source. Put the Insta-Glucose, a little bit at a time, between the cheeks (lips) and the gums and tell the child to swallow. If he/she can't swallow, lay the child down and turn the head to the side so the sugar (glucose) doesn't cause choking. You can help the sugar solution absorb by massaging the child's cheek.

If a low blood sugar (insulin reaction) or other problems occur, please call:

1. Parent _____ at: _____

2. _____ at: _____

3. _____ at: _____

MEALS, SNACKS AND INSULIN

The child must have meals and snacks on time. The schedule is as follows:

	Time	Food to Give	Insulin to Give
Breakfast	_____	_____	_____
Snack	_____	_____	_____
Lunch	_____	_____	_____
Snack	_____	_____	_____
Supper	_____	_____	_____
Snack	_____	_____	_____

Sometimes young children will not eat meals and snacks at exactly the time suggested. If this happens, DON'T PANIC! Set the food within the child's reach (in front of the TV set often works) and leave him/her alone. If the food hasn't been eaten in 10 minutes, give a friendly reminder. Allow about 30 minutes for meals.

BLOOD SUGARS

It may be necessary to check the blood sugar (Chapter 7) or ketones (Chapter 5).

The supplies we use are: _____

The supplies are kept: _____

Please record the results of any blood sugars or urine ketones in the log book.

Time:_____ Result: _____

(copy as needed)

INSULIN PUMPS

Many young children now receive their insulin via an insulin pump. The depth of knowledge about pumps will depend on the time of stay. At a minimum, you must be able to turn the pump off (or disconnect the tubing) with a low blood sugar and to turn it back on when the blood sugar rises. Also, if a very high blood sugar occurs (± ketones), a new infusion set may be needed (or a temporary shot of insulin). Parents often stay in close contact (when possible) to help advise.

If the stay is to be more than a few hours, it may be necessary to know how to approximate the amount of carbohydrates (carbs) to be eaten and to enter the value in the pump. If the blood sugar meter does not communicate automatically with the pump, the blood sugar value will also need to be entered. An insulin dose is then suggested by the pump and only needs to be accepted.

SIDE TRIPS

Please be sure that if the child is away from home, with you or with friends, extra snacks and a source of sugar are taken along.

OTHER CONCERNS: *Concerns that we have are:*

_____

_____

_____

_____

_____

_____

_____

_____

_____

_____

_____

_____

If there are any questions or if our child does not feel well or vomits, please call us or the other people listed above. Thank you.

(copy as needed)

KEEP THE
EMERGENCY LIST IN AN
EASY-TO-FIND PLACE.

BE PREPARED FOR ANYTHING WHEN
YOU'RE PLANNING TO CAMP OR VACATION.
SPECIAL PLANNING IS IMPORTANT FOR VACATIONS.

CHAPTER 27
VACATIONS AND CAMP

WHEN TRAVELING, WHAT SHOULD PLANNING INCLUDE?

• Insulin, blood sugar and ketone strips, glucagon and CGM sensors must be kept in a plastic bag in a cooler if traveling by car. All will spoil if they get above 90° F (32° C) or if they freeze.

• If the meter has been in a cold place, it should be brought to room temperature before doing a blood sugar.

• Car travel may result in higher blood/CGM glucose levels due to less activity. Extra basal and bolus insulin is sometimes given.

• Remember to take supplies for measuring ketones.

• Insulin should be carried on airplanes and not packed in "checked-in" luggage.

• It is important with airplane travel to have a vial of insulin with the pre-printed pharmacy label on the outside of the box. The glucagon should also be left in its original container. Carry supplies on-board in case a suitcase is lost. There have been no problems with taking insulin, insulin pumps or other diabetes supplies through security. Insulin pumps and continuous glucose monitors (CGM) should be worn and not put on the belt (x-ray) or exposed to a body scanner, as electronic components can be altered by x-ray. A travel letter from the diabetes doctor may also be required (including his/her phone number).

• Extras of everything should be carried by a second person when possible in case one carry-on is lost.

• Extra snacks (sugar [dextrose] tablets, granola bars, etc.) should be carried in case food is late or not available.

• Time changes within the U.S. are usually not a problem, but they must be considered if going overseas. Call your doctor or nurse for help with insulin adjustments if needed. For insulin pumps, the time in the pump is just reset.

• If traveling by plane and wearing an insulin pump, the high altitude sometimes causes pressure and extra insulin to be administered. Temporary basal rates or discontinuing insulin during pressure changes (maximum of two hours) is sometimes needed.

• If activity is to be increased during vacations, such as playing at the beach, fishing, hiking, going to an amusement park, etc., the insulin dose should be decreased.

CAMP

Diabetes camp is often the first chance for a child and parents to show they can survive without each other. Most camps have doctors and nurses present so that the children are safe. Getting to know other children with diabetes who are of a similar age can be very helpful. Most of all, camp should be fun!

If going to a non-diabetes camp (or school camp/outdoor lab):

• It is essential the camp nurse and cabin counselor know about diabetes (low blood sugars and what to do, high blood sugars and what to do, illness and what to do, etc.).

• Insulin changes for camp will need to be made by the child's diabetes doctor or nurse. Insulin dosages are often reduced by 20 or 30 percent – particularly for the first few days at camp.

• All diabetes supplies will need to be provided by the family.

• Phone numbers need to be provided to report blood sugars and receive insulin dose changes and for any emergency.

SWIMMING IS FUN . . .

. . . AND SO IS RIDING AN ELEPHANT.

CHAPTER 28
INSULIN PUMPS

THE PUMP

An insulin pump is a micro-computer (the size of a pager) worn externally that constantly provides insulin. Only rapid-acting insulin is used in pumps. Pumps have become more popular in recent years. Advantages and disadvantages of pumps are discussed in Chapter 28 in the larger book, "*Understanding Diabetes.*" In addition, a book "*Understanding Insulin Pumps and Continuous Glucose Monitors*" is available (see "Ordering Materials" in the back of this book). After reading one or both of these resources, the family may wish to discuss possible pump use with their diabetes care providers. If insurance will cover a continuous glucose monitor (CGM; Chapter 29), it may also be helpful to order this at the same time.

HOW IS INSULIN GIVEN BY THE PUMP?

The **basal** insulin dose provides a preset amount of insulin each hour. This can be changed at any time to fit the person's needs. This takes the place of long-acting insulins such as Lantus, Levemir or Tresiba.

A **bolus** insulin dose is entered/given by the person wearing the pump (or by an adult) each time food is eaten or if a high blood/CGM glucose level is found.

WHAT IS INVOLVED WHEN STARTING ON A PUMP?

- The first week (and for some, the first month) is the most difficult as the system is learned.

- At least four blood sugars per day must routinely be done prior to starting a pump.

- Carbohydrate counting (see Chapter 12) and correction factors (Chapter 22) are used to determine bolus doses.

- All pumps are now "smart pumps" and have insulin-to-carbohydrate (I/C) ratios and correction factors programmed into them (or into a linking meter) per the physician and family. Then, when a blood sugar and/or grams of carbohydrate to be eaten are entered, the pump suggests an appropriate insulin dose. This dose can be given as suggested or it can be changed.

- Bolus dosages for food are best taken 20 minutes before eating (unless the blood/CGM glucose level is low).

- When young children are treated with a pump, the parents are responsible for counting carbohydrates and giving the bolus insulin doses (see Chapter 19).

- Basal and bolus insulin doses are individualized for each person. The physician usually suggests initial basal rates, insulin to carbohydrate ratios and correction factors. These can then be altered as needed for different times of the day.

- Alternate basal rate patterns can also be

entered for special situations (extreme exercise, illness, etc.).

- Close contact with the healthcare-providers is essential.

- Our experience shows that children do well using an insulin pump if they and their parents are highly motivated.

- *The person with diabetes must be ready for the pump. It must not be just the parents (other than for very young children).*

THREE DIFFICULTIES SEEN WITH INSULIN PUMP USE

- Forgetting to give bolus insulin doses will result in a high HbA1c level.

- Not doing at least four blood sugars per day (or consistently wearing a CGM) may lead to a high HbA1c level.

- The cannula (tube) coming out from under the skin or kinking will cause blood/CGM glucose levels to rapidly rise. Remember,

only rapid-acting insulin, which is short-lasting, is used in a pump. Ketones begin to form after three hours with no insulin.

THREE ADVANTAGES OF INSULIN PUMP USE

- Insulin dosages can be finely tuned for different periods of the day.

- Insulin levels during and following exercise can be more safely managed.

- The possibility of combining with a CGM and the Threshold (Low Glucose) Suspend System offers safety in the prevention of hypoglycemia. This involves a CGM turning a pump off for up to two hours when the CGM detects a low blood sugar. Time spent with low blood sugars, particularly at night, is reduced as a result. The era of the "bionic" pancreas has now begun (see Chapter 30).

THE PERSON WITH DIABETES MUST WANT TO USE THE PUMP (NOT JUST THE PARENTS).

USING AN INSULIN PUMP
SOMETIMES INCREASES
ONE'S ENERGY.

FOOD IN MOUTH,
HAND ON PUMP!

CHAPTER 29
CONTINUOUS GLUCOSE MONITORING (CGM)

One of the major advances in the treatment of diabetes in recent years has been in the development of continuous glucose monitors (CGM). These devices give readings of subcutaneous (the tissue under the skin) glucose levels every five to ten minutes. This compares with finger-stick blood sugar (glucose) readings which are often done only four to six times each day. The subcutaneous CGM glucose values are approximately 10 minutes behind the blood sugar values. This is because the sugar must pass through the blood vessel wall into the subcutaneous space, and then the CGM system must determine the value. This delay is of almost no clinical significance with the frequency of CGM readings.

The purpose of this chapter is to present a brief overview of CGM. An entire book on Insulin Pumps and CGM is available for people wanting detailed information ("*Understanding Insulin Pumps and Continuous Glucose Monitors*" – see ordering materials in the back of this book). It is important to emphasize that, as with insulin pumps, the CGM technology is not for everyone. Some essential points are summarized below.

- The person (except for the very young) and not just the parents must want to use the CGM.

- Currently, blood sugar levels must still be done at least twice daily to calibrate the CGM (see below). They also must also be done anytime a low or high blood sugar is suspected, or if the CGM value is in question.

- The CGM values will not always match the blood sugar values.

- The more the CGM is worn, the more it can help.

THE COMPONENTS OF A CONTINUOUS GLUCOSE MONITOR (CGM)

The CGMs currently available in the U.S. all have three basic parts:

1. Sensor: As with the insulin pump, a small plastic probe is inserted (with the push of a button) under the skin. The sensor reads subcutaneous (not blood) glucose levels for the next five to seven days (it is often possible to make them last even longer).

2. Transmitter: The transmitter attaches to the sensor and sends the glucose reading to the receiver.

3. Receiver or Monitor: The receiver receives the glucose readings from the transmitter. It is a mini-computer that can record and save weeks of glucose information. The Medtronic system has the receiver within the insulin pump (for pumpers).

INITIATING CGM THERAPY

As with initiation of an insulin pump, various clinics will have different protocols for beginning CGM therapy. The criteria for deciding who is ready to begin CGM therapy are similar to those discussed for starting an insulin pump (Chapter 28). Many clinics also have CGM systems for short-term and diagnostic use.

SOME ADVANTAGES OF CGM

1. **Glucose levels**: Knowing glucose levels every few minutes throughout the day, particularly after meals and during the night, can be a great help.

2. **Trend graphs**: The trend graphs show the direction a glucose level is going (in contrast to a single point in time for a blood sugar level).

3. **Warning alarms**: The alarms for high and low glucose levels can help to prevent episodes of DKA or hypoglycemia.

4. **Preventing severe hypoglycemia:** The first part of the "bionic" pancreas (Chapter 30) was approved for the U.S. by the FDA in September, 2013. It is called the "Artificial Pancreas Device System," or the 530-G Threshold (Low Glucose) Suspend System. This involves the CGM turning off an insulin pump for up to two hours when a low glucose level is detected if the person has not responded to alarms. If the person/family does respond, they can turn the pump back on at any time.

5. **Reduced finger pokes:** Fewer blood sugars are generally needed.

6. **Lower HbA1c:** If worn consistently (e.g., six days per week), HbA1c levels usually decrease.

SOME DIFFICULT ISSUES WITH CGM

1. **Adhesive issues:** Adhesion issues for the sensor/transmitter are one of the two most frequent difficulties with CGM. For some people this is not a problem. For others, it is a major difficulty. The issues are discussed in detail in the Pump and CGM book.

2. **Calibration:** A second issue with CGM involves calibrating the system so that the CGM values are as accurate as possible and are matching the blood sugar values. Calibration involves doing a finger-stick blood sugar and entering it into the receiver, preferably at a time when the blood sugar is not rapidly changing.

3. **Alarms:** Some people are annoyed by the alarms for high and low glucose levels or for the need to do a calibration. Alarms can be set on higher or lower glucose levels to make them less frequent or on "vibrate." If bothersome, discuss with the diabetes care-providers.

4. **Comfort:** The sensors are gradually getting smaller.

5. **Cost:** Insurance coverage should be checked prior to ordering the CGM system. Coverage is gradually improving.

6. **Accuracy:** As with development of blood sugar meters, each new sensor version is more accurate. There will always be occasional sensors that do not function well.

SENSOR PLACEMENT AND ADHESION

Placement: Each CGM company has suggestions for where to place their sensors. In general, they can be worn on the back of the arm, the abdomen, hips, or buttocks. The selected area must have enough skin/fat to be able to pinch up a little bit with two fingers.

Adhesive use: There are many different adhesive wipes, tapes, and bandages that can help sensors to stick to skin. It is quite common for a person to use an adhesive wipe to treat the skin under the sensor, to then place the sensor on the skin, and finally to reinforce it with additional tape. Every person is different, and what works for one person may not work for others. Detailed suggestions are given in the Pump and CGM book.

CGM DATA

There are two main types of data that can be obtained from CGM usage: **Real-Time** and **Retrospective**. Real-time data refers to data available while wearing the CGM, such as a "trend-graph" showing a series of glucose values. Retrospective data refers to data from the past, most often downloaded using a computer. Both types of data are important and are explained in detail in the Pump and CGM book.

I FEEL SAFE
WEARING MY PUMP
AND CGM.

CHAPTER 30
THE "BIONIC" PANCREAS

The "bionic" or "artificial" pancreas (AP) refers to a combination of a continuous glucose monitor (CGM) and an insulin pump working together to increase, decrease, stop or start insulin administration as needed to control blood glucose levels. The CGM sends the glucose data to the receiver where mathematical formulas (algorithms) tell the pump how to regulate the insulin. Although the complete bionic pancreas is not yet available, it will likely be approved in stages.

The first stage of the bionic pancreas was approved outside the U.S. in 2009 and within the U.S. in 2013. It is likely that additional parts of the bionic pancreas will be approved over the next several years. The hurdles to overcome include:

• the difficulties with CGM glucose accuracy

• the need to develop computer algorithms for insulin delivery

• the need for a more rapid-acting insulin (ultra-rapid)

• the U.S. Food and Drug Administration needing to approve each step

• the need for more 'user-friendly' devices

To date, progress has continued to advance outside the U.S., and will likely come more slowly in the U.S.

STEP 1: THRESHOLD (OR LOW GLUCOSE) SUSPEND

The Threshold Suspend, (referred to outside the U.S. as Low Glucose Suspend [LGS]), a feature of the Medtronic Sensor Augmented Pump System, is already available within and outside the U.S. This requires use of the Medtronic 530G insulin pump and the Enlite sensor with the Medtronic CGM. Outside the U.S., the system uses the Paradigm VEO insulin pump and the Low Glucose Suspend feature. The Threshold Suspend system represents a major advancement in the development of the closed loop pancreas. The insulin pump is turned off for up to two hours if the CGM glucose value is below a set level (often 60 mg/dL or 3.3 mmol/L). The person can respond to the alarm, consume carbs, and turn the pump back on at any time during the two hours. This is what occurs in the majority of cases, particularly during the day. Most of the full two-hour suspensions (with alarms not responded to by the wearer) occur during sleep. This has been shown in multiple research reports to reduce time spent in hypoglycemia. There is also some evidence that wearing the Threshold Suspend System will reduce the number of lows. **Most important, it is an effective therapy to help prevent severe hypoglycemic episodes.**

Severe hypoglycemia is dangerous, and the ability to stop an insulin infusion from an insulin pump with a low CGM glucose level, or even better, with an impending low CGM glucose level (see STEP 2), is very important. Approximately half of severe hypoglycemic events in adults and 75% in children occur during sleep. Thus, decreasing basal insulin or turning a pump off with actual or predicted hypoglycemia during the night is extremely valuable. The pump can be turned off for two hours without danger of ketone formation. The System warning alarms are also valuable, but frequently do not awaken people during the night.

STEP 2: PREDICTED LOW GLUCOSE SUSPEND (PLGS)

It is obviously better to prevent hypoglycemia than to treat it (e.g., stopping insulin pump delivery before hypoglycemia occurs). In addition to the person feeling better, the body does not reduce stores of adrenaline (epinephrine). By predicting that the glucose level is going to become low, the pump can decrease or stop insulin to prevent the low, or at least to reduce the duration of the low sugar level. Current overnight data suggests a glucose level must be below 60 mg/dL (3.3 mmol/L) for over two hours before a hypoglycemic seizure would occur. Use of the PLGS (and of the LGS) can greatly reduce the risk that this would occur. Although this feature is not yet commercially available, it will likely be the second part of the bionic pancreas to be approved.

STEP 3: OVERNIGHT GLUCOSE CONTROL

It is likely the third part of the bionic pancreas will involve control of overnight insulin administration and sugar levels. This is much easier than management of daytime values, when food intake, exercise, stress and other factors cause frequent changes in glucose levels. In addition, recent evidence suggests the morning fasting glucose level to be the most important of the day. This is likely because the liver releases less sugar when adequate insulin is available.

STEP 4: THE COMPLETE ARTIFICIAL PANCREAS (AP)

Although the fully automated AP system requires more research, it will only gradually become available. The person will likely push a button to do a double insert of the CGM sensor and the insulin pump catheter (very close to each other). The pump will then handle all insulin administration based on the CGM glucose levels. Prior to a fully automated AP, until ultra-rapid insulins are available, people may need to still give pre-meal insulin boluses prior to eating.

With the AP, sugar control will be greatly improved, with reduced danger of severe hypoglycemia. Although people will need to remain diligent in self-care, overall management will be safer and easier.

CHAPTER 31
PREGNANCY AND DIABETES

Pregnancy is possible for women with diabetes who do not have severe problems with complications. Pregnancy is discussed in more detail in the book "*Management of Diabetes in Adults*" (see ordering materials in the back of this book).

WHAT IS IMPORTANT WHEN THINKING ABOUT GETTING PREGNANT?

• Pregnancy should be <u>planned</u>.

• The best sugar control possible should be achieved before and during pregnancy. The HbA1c should be below 6.5 percent (48 mmol/mol). (The ADA recommends below 6.0 percent [42 mmol/mol]).

• The risk of a miscarriage as well as birth defects in the baby are less if blood sugar/CGM values are normal or near normal when the pregnancy begins. This is why we recommend planning a pregnancy with tight sugar control achieved first.

• Folic acid should be taken for three months before the pregnancy to also help prevent birth defects.

HOW CAN THE BEST SUGAR CONTROL BE ACHIEVED?

Intensive insulin therapy is usual during pregnancy. This includes:

• an insulin pump or frequent insulin shots

• frequent blood sugar checks (eight to ten a day) or CGM

• paying close attention to nutrition

• frequent contact with the healthcare team

The target values for blood sugar/CGM values are lower than usual and are given in the Table in Chapter 15 of the above referenced book "*Management of Diabetes in Adults.*"

Clinic visits are also more frequent, usually every two to four weeks.

WHAT ABOUT COMPLICATIONS AND PREGNANCY?

Kidney damage is usually not a problem during pregnancy unless already present before the pregnancy. Medicines used to prevent kidney damage called "ACE-inhibitors" should not be taken during pregnancy. This medicine could cause birth defects in the baby.

The eyes should be checked more often during pregnancy (at least every three months). If moderate damage is already present, this may get worse during pregnancy.

117

GESTATIONAL DIABETES

Gestational diabetes is diabetes that develops as a result of the stress of the pregnancy. Regular exercise and diet are important.

- After diagnosis, care during pregnancy is similar to that of a person who had diabetes prior to pregnancy.

- Gestational diabetes usually goes away after pregnancy. There is an increased risk of developing type 2 diabetes later in life.

GOOD SUGAR CONTROL PRIOR TO PREGNANCY IS ESSENTIAL!

CHAPTER 32
RESEARCH AND DIABETES

THE FIVE SUBJECTS PEOPLE ASK MOST ABOUT ARE:

A Cure

Pancreas or islet transplantation is already possible. The problem is that the strong medicines necessary to prevent rejection can be more harmful than having diabetes. Many new medicines are being tried, but it is still early. Fortunately, advances are being made in the intensive management of diabetes, providing this as an alternative to surgical transplantation and a life of suppressing the immune system.

A "Bionic" Pancreas

The term "bionic" pancreas refers to a continuous glucose monitor (CGM) sending glucose data to a mini-computer which then instructs an insulin pump to give more or less insulin. Parts of the bionic pancreas are becoming available separately (see Chapter 30). The first part, the ability to turn off an insulin pump with a low glucose value, was approved by the FDA in September, 2013. Other features, such as turning off a pump when the CGM predicts a low glucose level, will likely follow.

A book, "*Understanding Insulin Pumps and Continuous Glucose Monitors*" is available (see ordering materials in the back of this book).

Prevention of Type 1 Diabetes (see www.diabetestrialnet.org)

• Several trials are currently under way.

• In the U.S., people can call 1-800-425-8361 to find out where to go for a free TrialNet antibody screening. Much is being learned to better design studies to prevent diabetes in the future.

• Four biochemical islet cell antibodies (Chapter 3) are being used to determine if the autoimmune process has begun. If it has, research trials are enrolling people in studies to try to reverse the process and prevent diabetes.

• Prevention trials are now focused on:

  ~ preventing the autoimmune process from starting

  ~ reversing the autoimmune process to prevent diabetes

  ~ stopping further damage to the islets after diabetes has been diagnosed

Prevention of Type 2 Diabetes

• This has already been shown to be possible.

• It usually involves eating less, exercising more, and losing weight.

• It is discussed in Chapter 4 of "*Understanding Diabetes.*"

Prevention of Complications

• Diabetes complications are decreasing through attention being paid to the following:

~ better sugar control

~ exercise, a healthy diet and optimal body weight

~ blood pressure control

~ not smoking

~ normal levels of blood lipids (e.g., cholesterol, LDL and HDL cholesterol)

~ yearly eye exams and urine microalbumin levels (to check the kidneys). These are essential after five years of diabetes for people who have had type 1 diabetes for five or more years, starting at age 10 years or at puberty, whichever is first (see Chapter 23). Families may need to help remind their diabetes care-provider to make sure these are done each year.

THE "BIONIC" PANCREAS IS HERE!

FINDING THE CURE

SOMEDAY THERE WILL BE
A CURE FOR DIABETES!

PUBLICATIONS ORDER FORM

Additional copies of "*A First Book for Understanding Diabetes*" as well as other diabetes publications may be ordered by using this form, by calling the Children's Diabetes Foundation at 303-863-1200, or by visiting our website at www.ChildrensDiabetesFoundation.org

Children's Diabetes Foundation
4380 South Syracuse Street, Suite 430 • Denver, CO 80237

Name: _____

Address: _____

City, State, ZIP: _____

Phone: _____ Email: _____

Quantity	Item	Price	Total
	A First Book for Understanding Diabetes, 13th Edition Presents the essentials from *Understanding Diabetes*	$13.00*	
	Un Primer Libro Para Entender La Diabetes 13th Edition (Available in late 2014)	$13.00*	
	Un Primer Libro Para Entender La Diabetes 11th Edition	$5.00*	
	Understanding Diabetes – "The Pink Panther Book" 13th Edition (Available in early 2015)	$20.00*	
	Understanding Diabetes – "The Pink Panther Book" 12th Edition	$10.00*	
	Understanding Insulin Pumps and Continuous Glucose Monitors 2nd Edition	$10.00*	
	Management of Diabetes in Adults 1st Edition	$15.00*	
	DIABETES: A History of a Center and a Patient	$15.00*	
	SHIPPING AND HANDLING: 5.00 per book for orders of 1-9 books 2.00 per book for orders of 10 books and over	Shipping and Handling	
		TOTAL	

* Prices subject to change.

☐ Please include me on the Children's Diabetes Foundation mailing list.
☐ Check enclosed payable to: Children's Diabetes Foundation
☐ Visa ☐ MasterCard ☐ Discover ☐ AmEx
Card # _____ Exp. Date _____

All orders must be paid in full before we can mail. Books are mailed USPS or Ground UPS
Allow one to three weeks for delivery.
Canadian and Foreign Purchasers: Please include sufficient funds to equal U.S. currency exchange rates.
For quantity order pricing and additional information call 303-863-1200 or visit our websit
www.ChildrensDiabetesFoundation.org

Barbara Davis Center for Diabetes
University of Colorado Denver
Mail Stop A140, Building M20
1775 Aurora Court
Aurora, CO 80045
303-724-2323 • Fax 303-724-6779
www.BarbaraDavisCenter.org

Children's Diabetes Foundation at Denver, Colorado
www.ChildrensDiabetesFoundation.org

Children With Diabetes
www.ChildrenwithDiabetes.com

Juvenile Diabetes Research Foundation
www.jdrf.org

American Diabetes Association
www.diabetes.org

PUBLICATIONS ORDER FORM

Additional copies of *"A First Book for Understanding Diabetes"* as well as other diabetes publications may be ordered by using this form, by calling the Children's Diabetes Foundation at 303-863-1200, or by visiting our website at www.ChildrensDiabetesFoundation.org

Children's Diabetes Foundation
4380 South Syracuse Street, Suite 430 • Denver, CO 80237

Name: _____

Address: _____

City, State, ZIP: _____

Phone: _____ Email: _____

Quantity	Item	Price	Total
	A First Book for Understanding Diabetes, 13th Edition Presents the essentials from *Understanding Diabetes*	$13.00*	
	Un Primer Libro Para Entender La Diabetes 13th Edition (Available in late 2014)	$13.00*	
	Un Primer Libro Para Entender La Diabetes 11th Edition	$5.00*	
	Understanding Diabetes – "The Pink Panther Book" 13th Edition (Available in early 2015)	$20.00*	
	Understanding Diabetes – "The Pink Panther Book" 12th Edition	$10.00*	
	Understanding Insulin Pumps and Continuous Glucose Monitors 2nd Edition	$10.00*	
	Management of Diabetes in Adults 1st Edition	$15.00*	
	DIABETES: A History of a Center and a Patient	$15.00*	
	SHIPPING AND HANDLING: 5.00 per book for orders of 1-9 books 2.00 per book for orders of 10 books and over	Shipping and Handling	
		TOTAL	

* Prices subject to change.

☐ Please include me on the Children's Diabetes Foundation mailing list.
☐ Check enclosed payable to: Children's Diabetes Foundation
☐ Visa   ☐ MasterCard   ☐ Discover   ☐ AmEx

Card # _____ Exp. Date _____

All orders must be paid in full before we can mail. Books are mailed USPS or Ground UPS
Allow one to three weeks for delivery.
Canadian and Foreign Purchasers: Please include sufficient funds to equal U.S. currency exchange rates.
For quantity order pricing and additional information call 303-863-1200 or visit our website at www.ChildrensDiabetesFoundation.org

WEBSITES

Barbara Davis Center for Diabetes
University of Colorado Denver
Mail Stop A140, Building M20
1775 Aurora Court
Aurora, CO 80045
303-724-2323 • Fax 303-724-6779
www.BarbaraDavisCenter.org

Children's Diabetes Foundation at Denver, Colorado
www.ChildrensDiabetesFoundation.org

Children With Diabetes
www.ChildrenwithDiabetes.com

Juvenile Diabetes Research Foundation
www.jdrf.org

American Diabetes Association
www.diabetes.org